QuickBooks
FOR
CONTRACTORS

PRESENTED BY:
CRAIG M. KERSHAW, CPA, MBA

QuickBooks for Contractors

For permission requests, write to:
The CFO Source, LLC
5515 Hudson Drive
Eldersburg, MD 21784
www.cfosource.net

Ordering Information:
Quantity sales. Special discounts are available on quantity purchases by corporations, associations, and others. Orders by U.S. trade bookstores and wholesalers. For details, contact the publisher at the address above.

ISBN: 978-0-9977388-0-3

Main category—Business & Economics > Bookkeeping
Other category—Business & Economics > Accounting

Printed in the United States of America
First Edition

Table of Contents

About the Author

Craig Kershaw, CPA, MBA is the managing partner of The CFO Source, a Baltimore based consulting firm that provides senior level financial expertise to small and medium size businesses. With over 20 years of experience at the CFO and Controller level in transportation, construction, and service industries, he has worked with medium size businesses and Fortune 500 corporations, demonstrating excellence across the full range of financial management responsibilities—financing, treasury, accounting, risk management, information technology, and QuickBooks training. Craig is experienced in all levels of financial and accounting software, from QuickBooks to custom systems used in multi-billion dollar operations.

A Certified QuickBooks Pro Advisor since 2009, Mr. Kershaw has helped numerous clients set up, trouble shoot, and fine tune their accounting. He teaches continuing professional education courses to members of the Maryland Association of CPAs using his QuickBooks series, and regularly contributes articles on QuickBooks functionality for the Maryland Construction Networks Networked and Connected newsletter. The CFO Source provides services to clients in the construction and contracting business, and the firm's guidance in their financial matters empowers them to more efficiently and effectively track job costs and profitability, manage backlog, improve estimating processes, and produce accurate financial statements. The CFO Source's clients receive training for tracking estimated costs versus actual, properly billing and collecting contract revenues, preparing percentage of completion information their lenders and sureties require, and worker's compensation reporting.

Craig's QuickBooks training series began as "how to" instructions for clients wanting to record specific transactions. In many cases, the guidance could not be found in more basic manuals. The growing list of real user "how to" solutions has developed into a series of books, allowing users to learn the breadth and scope of QuickBooks capabilities.

Chapter One

Overview of Functionality

Keeping track of the myriad of details necessary to run a successful contracting or construction business can seem like a daunting task. This book was designed to show contractors and their staff how to set up and use QuickBooks to manage the financial side of their business and maximize profitability. This accounting software has numerous features and reports, and can be customized to fit each contractor's unique situation. Knowing what these features are and getting the most out of QuickBooks can make a significant difference in the financial health and overall success of your business.

What Can QuickBooks Do for the Contractor?

- Generate Profit and Loss (P&L) Statements and Balance Sheets tailored for your business and put you in the best light for banks and sureties by giving you the ability to track the financial health of your company.
- Extensive reporting on profitability:

    1. P & L by job
    2. Summary job profitability reports
    3. Detailed job profitability reports including estimate to actual

- Allow you to prepare detailed estimates for presentation to customers.
- Job costing of all expense elements – payroll, fringes/burden, subcontractors, materials, equipment, insurances, and overhead.
- Compare actual job costs against estimated costs with variances as jobs progress.
- Complete payroll processing:

    - Track/charge employee time to jobs
    - Import time from third party time clock systems
    - Generate paychecks and direct deposits
    - Charge jobs for payroll taxes, fringes, and overhead
    - Tracking of workers' compensation by state and class code
    - Prepare weekly certified payroll reports

- Online tax filings and payments
- Emailing or online availability of deposit advices for employees, eliminating the need to hand out paychecks

- Bill customers and track collections – deposits, progress billings, retention.
- Process purchase orders and pay invoices for subcontractors and vendors.
- Track equipment costs by piece of equipment and allocation of costs to jobs.
- For government contractors, create cost "pools" of indirect costs for allocation to jobs.
- Track the general liability and workers' compensation insurance expiration dates of subcontractors.
- Inventory of commonly used materials and costing to jobs.
- Generate reports from which percentage completion accounting can be calculated.

Profit and Loss Statement Considerations

One of the hallmarks of success for a contracting firm is having a steady stream of projects contracted at prices that create profit margins. Knowing the level of profitability on past jobs and using that information to bid on future work is crucial to reaching and maintaining that goal.

Each company has a unique set of costs the managers must understand thoroughly to make appropriate decisions during any project or job. For many subcontractors, labor and workers' compensation are critical; for others, material costs and subcontractor payments drive success; and yet for others, it's equipment and fuel.

Setting up your Profit and Loss statement must take into account your company's unique costs and measure those costs against jobs to determine profitability. We recommend that contractor's set up their Profit and Loss statements so they can readily see the direct costs of jobs and corresponding gross profit. Consider the following:

- Set up the direct costs tracked against jobs in the same format that you use to prepare your cost estimates. This gives you the ability to compare "apples to apples."
- QuickBooks has the functionality to track costs at different levels of detail in different reports. The QuickBooks Profit and Loss statement is best suited for fairly broad categories, while the Job Estimate to Actual reporting is more appropriate for reporting at the detail level, to include variances from estimate. The P & L uses QuickBooks "Accounts," while the detailed reports utilize QuickBooks "Items."
- For those companies with large costs that are not easily charged directly to jobs (i.e. equipment costs like fuel, ownership costs, repairs) consider an equitable allocation approach such as operator hours, and track whether over or under applied.
- Realize that not all costs are worth the time to track by job.

QuickBooks's standard P & L is easily modified for use by contractors. Using QuickBooks's three "Costs/Expense" account types, the contractor can track job specific costs, overhead costs, and non-recurring/extraordinary costs. We suggest the following:

Type of Expenses	QuickBooks Account Type
Direct Job Costs	Cost of Goods Sold
Overhead and Indirect Costs	Expenses
Non-recurring Costs	Other Expenses

Balance Sheet Considerations

There are several accounts that may need to be set up for handling accounting that is unique to the construction industry. Any that do not apply to your firm do not need to be set up. Below is a list of these accounts, comments on usage, and the QuickBooks account type suggested.

Retention Receivable – The amount owners and general contractors hold back each billing (typically 10%) as retention that is not paid until job completion. It's suggested that these be set up with the account type "Other Current Receivable." Further discussion on the use of QuickBooks for retention accounting is in Chapter Seven.

Percentage Completion Accounting – for contractors who are required to do this accounting, two accounts will need to be set up as follows:

- **Costs and Estimated Earnings in Excess of Billings** – also referred to as "Underbillings"; set up with the account type "Other Current Asset"
- **Billings in Excess of Costs and Estimated Earnings** – also referred to as "Overbillings"; set up with the account type "Other Current Liability"

Deposits Payable – If your firm collects deposits in advance of performing work; set up using the "Other Current Liability" account type.

Determining the Level of Detail to Track

QuickBooks has the functionality to track a significant amount of job cost details and produce a myriad of reports. Some companies desire detailed information and are willing to invest time and effort in recording and analyzing the data. For other companies, summary level information is really all that is needed, and the cost to create the details would require more effort to input than the information would be worth. Each company must balance meeting its information needs with the effort and cost to generate it.

There are two primary levels of reporting on the details of individual job profitability, and each is described below along with the level of data processing necessary to produce the report.

Profit and Loss by job – a P&L statement can be generated for each job

- This report shows actual revenues and expenses only.
- Transactions for customer billing and expenses must be assigned to a Customer:Job to appear on the reporting. Setting up Customer:Job codes will be covered in Chapter Two.
- Revenues are recorded as invoices to customers using Customer:Job codes.
- Expenses can be recorded through QuickBooks payroll as vendor bills using the Expenses tab, or with journal entries.

Job Estimates versus Actuals Detail – this report allows for the tracking of estimates versus actual expenses. QuickBooks can be set up to track each component or phase of a job starting with plans and building permits, and progressing to labor, materials, subcontractors, equipment rentals, etc.

- This report shows both actual and estimated revenues and expenses.
- This reporting is driven by the use of item codes in QuickBooks. Contractors utilizing this approach can develop a detailed list of item codes customized to their business's job cost structure.
- Transactions for customer billing and expenses must be assigned a Customer:Job to appear on the reporting.
- Expenses must be recorded utilizing items codes, either through QuickBooks payroll or the items tab when recording vendor bills. Journal entries cannot be utilized.

The two primary reports that QuickBooks generates are shown below, utilizing the same sample job. Assumptions:

The company bid on a project to replace a kitchen for a lump sum of $15,000.

The company estimated the direct cost to complete the job is $10,450, while actual costs are $14,375.

Below is the P&L for the job, indicating that the expenses far exceeded the estimate. Note that the job did not perform to estimate, but it is difficult to pinpoint the exact reason for the problem.

Quality-Built Construction
Profit & Loss
January 2020

	Jan 20
▼ Ordinary Income/Expense	
▼ Income	
4110 · Construction Income	15,000.00
Total Income	15,000.00
▼ Cost of Goods Sold	
5200 · Job Labor Costs	1,900.00
5300 · Materials	7,850.00
5400 · Subcontractors	3,300.00
5950 · Other Job Costs	1,325.00
Total COGS	14,375.00
Gross Profit	625.00
Net Ordinary Income	625.00
Net Income	▶ 625.00 ◀

Below is the Job Estimates vs. Actuals Detail for the same job.

Quality-Built Construction
Job Estimates vs. Actuals Detail for James Smith:New Kitchen
All Transactions

	Est. Cost	Act. Cost	($) Diff.	Est. Revenue	Act. Revenue	($) Diff.
▼ Service						
▼ 01 Plans & Permits . (Plans & Permits)						
01.1 Plans (Plans)	500.00	950.00	450.00	0.00 ▶	0.00 ◀	0.00
01.2 Building Permits (Building Permit)	250.00	375.00	125.00	0.00	0.00	0.00
Total 01 Plans & Permits . (Plans & Perm...	750.00	1,325.00	575.00	0.00	0.00	0.00
▼ 02 Site Work (Site Work)						
02.10 Demo (Demolition)	750.00	0.00	-750.00	0.00	0.00	0.00
Total 02 Site Work (Site Work)	750.00	0.00	-750.00	0.00	0.00	0.00
07 Wall Framing (Wall Framing)	500.00	800.00	300.00	0.00	0.00	0.00
14 Plumbing (Plumbing)	750.00	1,450.00	700.00	0.00	0.00	0.00
16 Electrical & Lighting (Electrical & Ligh...	750.00	1,250.00	500.00	0.00	0.00	0.00
17 Insulation (Insulation)	0.00	600.00	600.00	0.00	0.00	0.00
18 Interior Walls (Interior Walls)	500.00	0.00	-500.00	0.00	0.00	0.00
20 Millwork & Trim (Millwork & Trim)	250.00	150.00	-100.00	0.00	0.00	0.00
21 Cabinets & Vanities (Cabinets & Vanities)	5,000.00	7,500.00	2,500.00	0.00	0.00	0.00
23 Floor Coverings (Floor Coverings)	750.00	350.00	-400.00	0.00	0.00	0.00
24 Paint (Painting)	500.00	750.00	250.00	0.00	0.00	0.00
25 Cleanup (Cleanup & Restoration)	250.00	200.00	-50.00	0.00	0.00	0.00
Total Service	10,750.00	14,375.00	3,625.00	0.00	0.00	0.00
▼ Other Charges						
Billing to Customer	0.00	0.00	0.00	15,000.00	15,000.00	0.00
Total Other Charges	0.00	0.00	0.00	15,000.00	15,000.00	0.00
TOTAL	10,750.00	14,375.00	3,625.00	15,000.00	15,000.00	0.00

This report allows the user to drill down and examine how each component of the estimate compares to actual. Clearly the cabinets and vanities ran significantly over estimate, but there was an overall trend to underestimate in several categories. Such information can be critical. For example, it may be determined that a change order is called for on the job, or that mistakes were made in the estimating process, as in this example, which can be avoided in the future.

As mentioned above, generating estimate to actual reporting involves additional steps:

- Item codes for each line of expense must be set up in QuickBooks.
- Estimates for jobs to be tracked must be prepared and input.
- All transactions, both revenue and expense must be processed using item codes.

Notes:

_____

_____

_____

_____

_____

_____

_____

_____

_____

_____

_____

_____

_____

_____

_____

_____

_____

_____

_____

_____

_____

_____

_____

_____

_____

_____

_____

_____

_____

_____

_____

_____

_____

_____

Chapter Two
Setting Up Jobs in QuickBooks

Jobs are a subset of Customers. A few key points:

- Customers and Jobs are set up in the Customer Center
- A customer must be set up first before a job under that customer can be created.
- Multiple jobs can be set up under one customer.
- Job titles are separated from customer names with a colon. For example, "Mr. & Mrs. Jones:Kitchen Remodel."
- The Jobs field is free form, and job numbers may or may not be used.

There are five data screens for the input of information about jobs and customers:

1. Address Info – mailing and email addresses, phone numbers
2. Payment Settings – customer account number, payment terms, credit card information, and credit limit
3. Sales Tax Setting – controls whether sales taxes are billed to customers
4. Additional Information – customer type, Rep (typically sales rep, but could be used for project manager) and custom information fields
5. Job Information – description and start/end dates

Below is a step-by-step of the set-up for Mr. and Mrs. Jones' kitchen remodel. First, the customer must be set up.

1. From the main menu in QuickBooks, select the Customers tab.

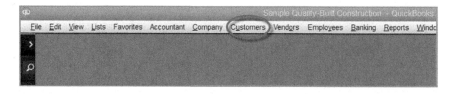

2. Select the Customer Center option, which will bring up a drop down menu. From the drop down menu, select Customer Center,

3. Once in the Customer Center, Select the New Customer & Job tab as shown below.

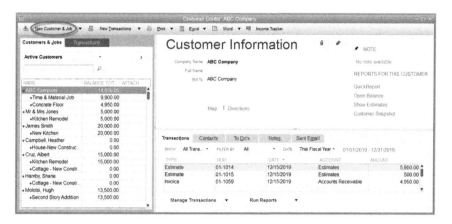

4. Selecting New Customer & Job will bring up three options:

   -New Customer
   -Add Job
   -Add multiple Customers:Jobs

5. Select New Customer to bring up Address Info (the first of five customer screens), input the appropriate information, and select the Payment Settings tab.

The Payment Settings screen is shown below. If payment terms different than the pre-set QuickBooks terms are desired, custom terms can be set up. Go to Lists, Customer & Vendor Profile lists, then select Terms List.

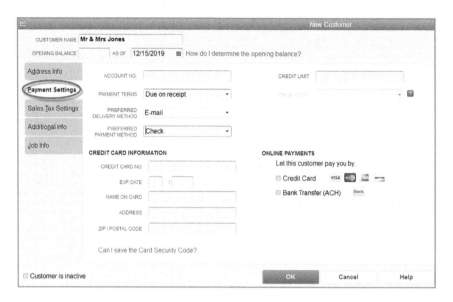

The Sales Tax Settings screen is shown below. If sales tax functionality is desired, it must first be set up in the Sales Tax Preferences section. To navigate to that section, begin at the main menu and select Edit, then Preferences, then Sales Tax. Once set up, you can designate if the customer is subject to sales tax and choose the appropriate state sales tax item code.

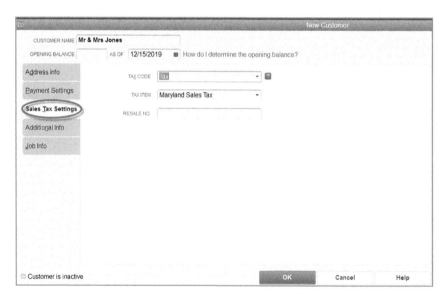

The Additional Info section is shown below. Additional names for the Customer Type and Rep (Sales Representative or alternatively, Project Manager) fields can be added on the fly or in the Lists area of the main menu.

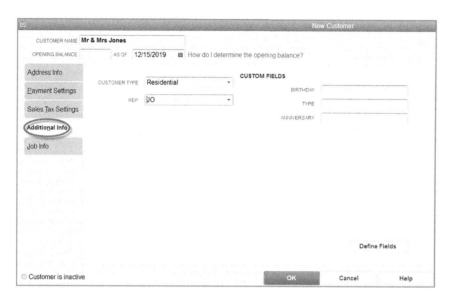

To set up a job underneath the customer, return to the main Customer Center Screen, click on the customer name in the list on the left, select New Customer & Job, then choose the Add Job option.

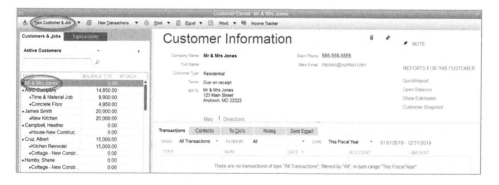

Input information on the New Job screen as shown below.

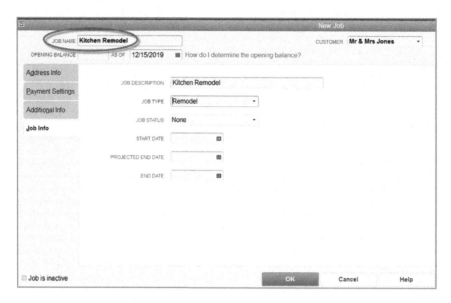

Address Info, Payment Settings, and Additional Info screens are also available for input, specific to the job. QuickBooks allows you to input or change information specific to jobs and separate from the information at the customer level. Note that the sales tax information cannot be added at the job level.

Notes:

_____
_____
_____
_____
_____
_____
_____
_____
_____
_____
_____
_____
_____
_____
_____
_____
_____
_____
_____
_____
_____
_____
_____
_____
_____
_____
_____
_____
_____
_____
_____
_____
_____
_____
_____
_____

Chapter Three
Customizing Item Codes

Overview

Item codes are an essential part of managing details in QuickBooks. They provide numerous ways to track and control revenues and expenses, and standardize transaction processing. Reports based on item codes provide a more detailed look at information than is usually desired in summary financial statements. Item codes can be customized to fit the unique needs of a business within the framework of the item code types available.

Common uses by contractors:

- Invoice customers
- Record expenses
- Create estimates for customers
- Track estimates versus actuals on jobs
- Track inventory quantities and values
- Categorize revenues and expenses into logical groupings

Item codes must be used for recording revenues and expenses in order to take full advantage of QuickBooks' cost reporting functionality, specifically for tracking estimates versus actuals. The codes provide a way to track detailed job level data that is typically too much information on a standard Profit and Loss statement. For example, contractors utilizing numerous types of materials may want to see these purchases broken out in detail, but only a single "Materials" line on their P&L. This is accomplished in the set-up of item codes, whereby each item code is "mapped" to post transactions to accounts on the Chart of Accounts.

Item Code Types

A key consideration in the set-up of items codes is the selection of an item code type. Item code types are fixed; that is, the user cannot change the title of an item type or add additional types. Each item code type has specific functionality and the proper selection is critical. Below are the key item code types useful for contractors, and a description of each. The descriptions are what will appear in QuickBooks when you select the respective item code type.

Item Code Type	Description/Functionality
Service	Use for services you charge for or purchase, like specialized labor, consulting hours, or professional fees.
Other Charge	Use for miscellaneous labor, material, or part charges, such as delivery charges, setup fees, and service charges.
Inventory Part	Use for goods you purchase, track as inventory, and resell.
Non Inventory Part	Use for goods you buy but don't track, like office supplies, or materials for a specific job that you charge back to the customers.
Subtotal	Use to total all items above it on a form, up to the last subtotal. Useful for applying a percentage discount or surcharge to many items.

It is suggested to use service item codes to track expenses and other charge codes to record invoicing for customers. This is important for two reasons:

1. Use of separate item code types provides for subtotaling of the two categories, so that total cost and total revenue can be looked at individually.
2. QuickBooks payroll will only post to service item codes.

Item codes should be customized to your business. Working with estimators, accountants should set up item codes so QuickBooks will produce reports for easy comparison of estimated versus actual costs.

QuickBooks Contractor Edition comes with item codes already set up for general contractors, which is shown in Appendix A. Notably missing from the list are item codes for what estimators refer to as "General Conditions," which are expenses typically used on all jobs such as job site trailers, trash removal, safety equipment, and permits. Appendix B shows a list of common general condition items.

For many subcontractors, the QuickBooks pre-defined item codes are not a fit for their business. These companies should delete or inactivate the pre-defined item codes and replace them with item codes customized for their particular line of work. For example, subcontractors may want to have separate item codes for each category of labor and material costs. Please refer to Appendix C for a sample item code list for subcontractors.

Sub item codes allow for subtotaling of broader areas of expense, such as where the sub item codes for straight time and overtime payroll will be subtotaled to Direct Labor. Similarly, multiple sub items of materials could be subtotaled to a total materials line.

Setting Up Item Codes

This is a critical part of getting the most out of QuickBooks because properly setting up item codes provides the user with powerful reports. During set up, you will:

- Determine the item code type.
- Give the item code a unique name.
- Give the item code a description. (optional)
- Determine if the item code is a sub of a main item code. (useful for subtotals)
- Map the item code to the Chart of Accounts for billing, payment, and inventory transactions where applicable.

Setting up item codes is a list function. From the main menu, select Lists, then Item List. This will bring up the item codes already set up in your QuickBooks, as shown below for a sample company.

Setting up or editing an item code is done by clicking on the arrow in the item box, in the bottom left of the item list (see above). This brings up a selection list of options, including setting up a new item code or editing an existing one. To edit an existing code, you must first highlight it in the list. The next section provides a sample set-up of a service item.

Set-Up of a Service Item Code

After selecting to set up a new item code, the user will be presented with this screen:

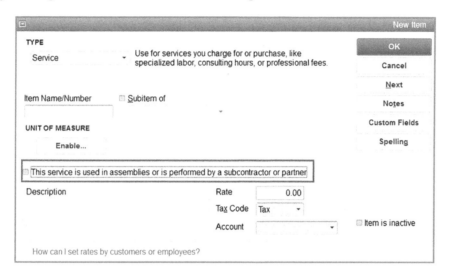

*** **VERY IMPORTANT** *** – if the item code is to be used for expense/payment transactions, the box labeled "This service is used in assemblies or is performed by a subcontractor or partner" must be checked. Checking this box will add a set of boxes that QuickBooks uses to map purchase transactions. Below is how the screen looks if the box is checked off:

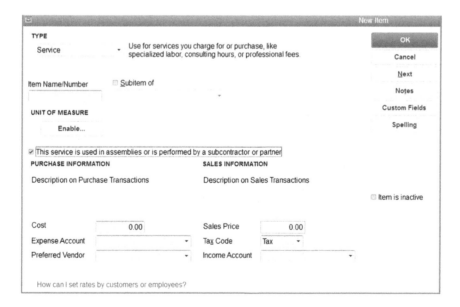

Complete the information as called for in each field, then click the OK button.

If this is not checked off and the item code is used for expense/payment transactions, these transactions will be posted to an account typically used for income/revenue transactions and appear as negative income.

Additional Information on Item Codes

For a more detailed discussion of item codes, please refer to the item code section in *QuickBooks for Advanced Users*. There, these additional topics are discussed:

- When to use item codes and when to use the Chart of Accounts
- Using the description field to speed up data entry
- Limitations on changing item code types
- Customizing the item code list to show account mapping
- Editing item codes that map to incorrect accounts
- Common item code problems and how to fix them

Notes:

_____

_____

_____

_____

_____

_____

_____

_____

_____

_____

_____

_____

_____

_____

_____

_____

_____

_____

_____

_____

_____

_____

_____

_____

_____

_____

_____

_____

_____

_____

_____

_____

_____

_____

_____

_____

Chapter Four

Creating and Using Estimates

Overview

Another hallmark of successful contracting companies is the preparation of accurate cost estimates. By tracking actual costs against estimates, they continuously monitor and improve their estimating process and skills, and in turn, profitability. Estimates can be prepared in QuickBooks or imported from Excel and/or other programs. QuickBooks estimates can be used as the proposal given to customers or only for internal purposes.

Recording estimates in QuickBooks is necessary in order to use the Estimate vs. Actuals reporting and to prepare progress billings. Estimates can be set up for either lump sum, unit pricing, or cost plus billing. Estimates can be customized as to what information appears, such as company logos, messages, and order of information.

Before an estimate can be set up, first the customer and job need to be set up. Refer to Chapter Two for step by step instructions on setting these up.

To bring up a blank estimate in QuickBooks:

1. From the main menu, go to Customers.
2. Select Create Estimates. This will bring up the blank estimate screen as shown below.
3. Select a Customer:Job from the drop down menu to begin the estimate.

The next step is to determine how you want to set up the estimate with regard to lines for expenses and revenue. QuickBooks can accommodate either a line for each item of cost with a markup, or one line for the total lump sum billing for the job and multiple lines for cost. How your estimates are prepared and how you need to bill customers may have a bearing on how you set up the estimate.

Showing Multiple Lines for Revenue

In some cases, an estimate of cost is determined for each line item of expense, and a profit factor added to each line. Subsequent billing is done on a line by line basis in progress billing while construction is under way. For example, in the construction of a building, separate lines may be developed for excavation, foundation, framing, plumbing, and so on, and billing is done accordingly.

Below is an estimate for an excavation and concrete job showing the separate lines for cost, markup, and the amount that will be billed for each part of the job.

A few pointers:

- Each line in the estimate is created by first choosing an appropriate item code.
- The quantity field can be used to multiply by unit prices to get a total cost, or the total can be input and no quantities shown. In the example, concrete cost was estimated at 20 yards multiplied by $25 per yard for a total estimated cost of $500, and excavation was estimated at a cost of $1,500 with no quantities shown.
- The amount shown in the Total field is the sum of the line by line information, providing the total cost estimate for the job; it is not a manual input field.
- The markup and revenue columns are both input fields, but each can drive the other. For example, in the first line for plans, inputting $250 in the Markup column will make the Revenue $450 (cost of $200, plus markup of $250). If, however, on the same line, the markup was blank and $450 was input into the revenue line, the markup would then show as $200.
- Markups can be input as a set dollar value or as percentages, as shown for excavation.
- When quantities are used, unit cost and pricing can be done using the amounts set up for each item code as shown below.

Unit cost and pricing set-up for item codes:

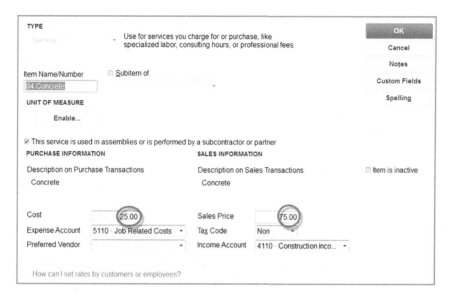

Showing Single Line for Revenue

In some cases, a total estimated cost is developed based on detailed calculations, then profit and overhead percentages are applied to come up with a lump sum estimate to use as the bid for the job. In a lump sum approach, you may want to only see one billing line for revenue, but many lines for each component of cost. For example, the billing may be such that progress billing is called for, but only based on the total contract. The estimate in QuickBooks can be structured to accommodate this.

As with any estimate, the customer and job must be created first.

Below is an estimate prepared with one line for the revenue, but multiple lines for the expenses. Several things need to be entered differently than on the multiple revenue line estimate.

- The total amount of the contract value—in this example, $15,000—is entered under one item code. On this line, nothing is entered in the Estimate column (which is where costs are normally entered), and the contract value is entered in the Markup column, which then carries over to the revenue line.
- Since the remaining lines in the estimate are only for costs, the cost figures need to also be entered as negative markup, which will make the revenue zero for these lines.

It's important to understand how the two different estimates will show when running the Job Estimates vs. Actuals Detail report. The reports are shown below for both examples.

Multiple Lines for Revenue:

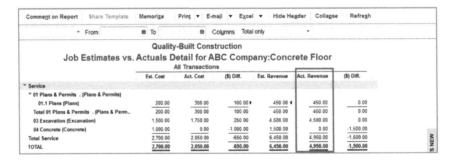

Single Line for Revenue – in this approach, the revenue only shows on the first line while the cost items do not appear in the revenue column

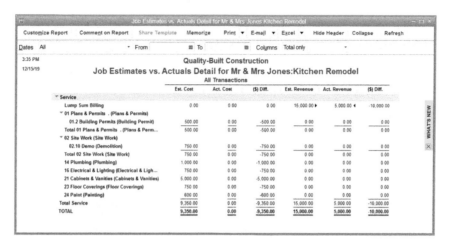

Notes:

Chapter Five

Vendor/Subcontractor Transactions

Recording Vendor Bills to Jobs

Recording bills payable to suppliers or subcontractors is done in the Vendor section of QuickBooks. From the main menu, select Vendors, then select Enter Bills to bring up the Enter Bills screen. Charging a bill to a job can be done with either the Expenses tab or the Items tab. Below is an example of the same bill done with both methods:

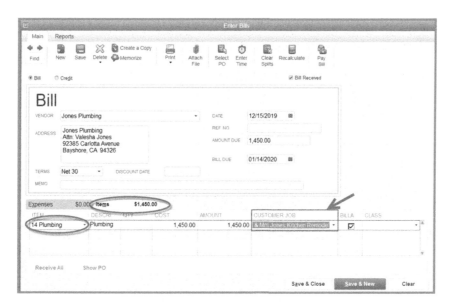

In the above example, an item code is used. Note that the items tab was selected, an appropriate item code for the nature of the expense was chosen, and the Customer:Job to which the bill applied was selected.

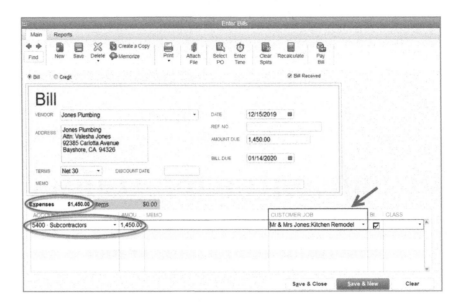

Above is the same bill recorded using the Expenses tab. Note there is no change on the Customer:Job information.

Both methods will record the bill for later payment and record the expense to the correct account. The main reason to record the bill in the item code tab instead of the expense tab is to enable the use of QuickBooks estimate to actual reporting.

Recording Vendor Refunds

While a refund received from a vendor can be recorded in the Banking "Make Deposits" area, this section of QuickBooks doesn't allow for recording the transaction at the item code level. Further, the user must decide whether to use the Vendor name or the Customer:Job name to apply the credit, but cannot choose both. Either selection is not ideal—if the Vendor name is used, the refund won't be shown as a reduction in any particular job; if the Customer:Job name is chosen, the cash received will be shown in the Customer Center as a cash receipt when in fact the cash came from a vendor.

An alternative approach is to use a "zero-dollar" bill in the Vendor section to record the deposit. With this approach, the refund can be shown as a reduction in the cost of a particular job at either the item code level or the expense level. Additionally, the refund can be recorded under the appropriate vendor and credited to the job the refund relates to. The end result in the accounts will be the same – a debit to a cash account and a credit to the desired expense account.

To demonstrate, we will assume the following situation:

Materials were purchased from XYZ Material Company for $3,500, and charged to the Tedford, Dan:Addition job. After delivery, some materials were found to be defective and XYZ Material Company sent a refund check for $500.

Below is how the original bill for $3,500 was recorded, with item code 12 Door & Trim.

Recording the $500 refund is a two-step process. Begin at the main menu and select Vendors, then Enter Bills, and select XYZ Material Company from the drop down vendor menu. In the expenses section, choose the appropriate bank account and enter $500, as shown below. It is not necessary to input the related job information in the Customer:Job field for the cash deposit part of the transaction.

For the second step, click on the Items tab, and enter the item code and Customer:Job from the transaction related to the refund. Enter the $500 in the amount field *as a negative number*.

This causes the bill amount to become zero as shown in the completed second screen below. Clicking on Save and Close completes the transaction.

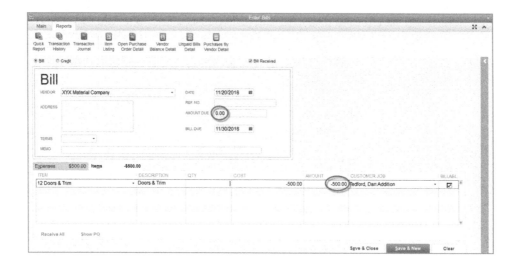

Below is a transaction journal for the zero-dollar bill used to record the deposit. Note that there is no impact on accounts payable.

As shown below, the zero-dollar bill is marked Paid and will not appear later as an open bill in the Vendors Pay Bills screen.

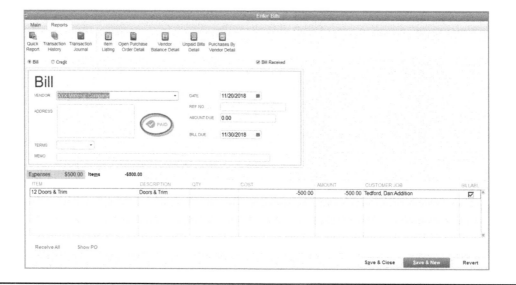

This approach can have numerous variations. For example, if item code detail is not desired, a second line on the expenses tab can be used to record the $500 deduction in an expense account. Yet another use would be to record a refund for an inventory purchase with negative amounts for not just the dollar amounts, but quantities as well.

Tracking Subcontractor Insurance Expiration Dates

General contractors should track their subcontractor's insurance expiration dates to make sure coverages do not lapse. Such lapses could result in the general contractor being liable for claims in the event of an injury or other type of accident caused by the subcontractor. Expiration dates for workers' compensation and general liability insurances can be entered in the Vendor Center.

From the main menu, select Vendors, then Vendor Center, which brings up the screen below. Select the desired vendor from the list on the left and click on the edit tab.

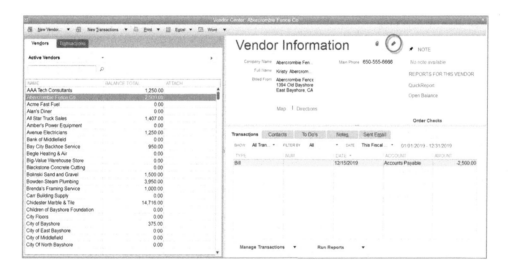

This will bring up the Edit Vendor screen. Select the Additional Info tab where the insurance expiration dates for workers' compensation and general liability insurances can be input.

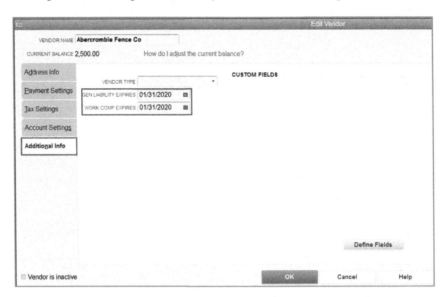

QuickBooks will not allow the entry of expiration dates in the past, and will display this message if the date is not in the future:

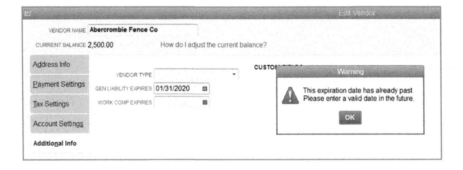

Once a subcontractor's expiration dates are entered, QuickBooks will give the user a warning when a bill is entered for a subcontractor whose insurance has expired, as shown below. Entry can still be made, however. No such warning is given when printing checks for vendors with expired insurance.

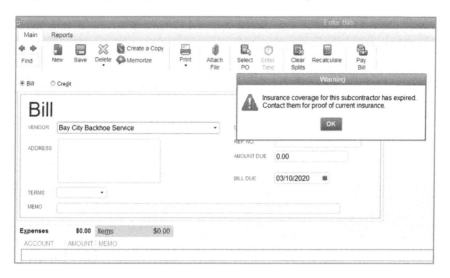

QuickBooks does not have a canned report showing vendor and insurance expiration dates, but the Vendor Contact list can be customized to show this information. From the main menu, select Reports, List, then Vendor Contact List, which will bring up the report below.

Clicking on the Customize Report tab in the report will bring up the Modify Report screen, where the insurance expiration fields can be selected in the Display tab of the screen. Other fields can be selected or not, depending on what is desired in the report.

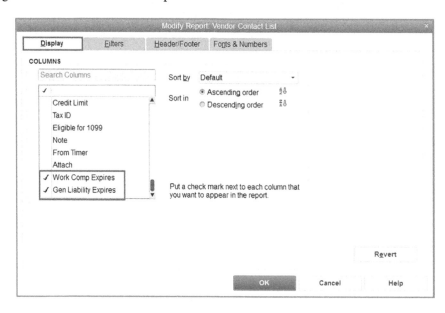

The report header can be customized to change the title of the report from "Vendor Contact List" to "Subcontractor Insurance Expiration Dates." This is done in the Header/Footer section of the Modify Report screen in the Report Title area.

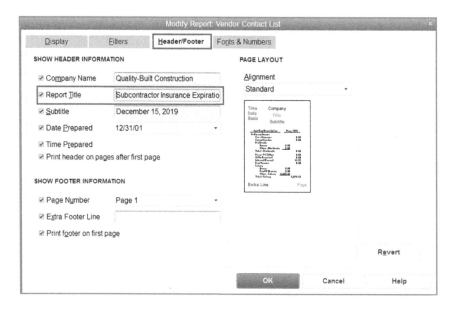

Below is the modified report:

		Quality-Built Construction		
		Subcontractor Insurance Expiration Dates		
		December 15, 2019		
Vendor	Main Phone	Primary Contact	Work Comp Expires	Gen Liability Expires
AAA Tech Consultants	650-555-1968	Mike Balak		
Abercrombie Fence Co	650-555-6666	Kristy	01/31/2020	01/31/2020
Acme Fast Fuel				
Alan's Diner		Alan Sun		
All Star Truck Sales	415-555-3418			
Amber's Power Equipment	650-555-6414	Amber		
Avenue Electricians	650-555-2684	Colleen Garton	10/31/2020	07/31/2020
Bank of Middlefield				
Bay City Backhoe Service	415-555-7826	Barb Caylor	05/31/2020	04/30/2020
Begle Heating & Air		Doug Begle	11/30/2020	02/29/2020
Big-Value Warehouse Store				
Blackstone Concrete Cutting	415-555-1368	Paula Easley		
Bolinski Sand and Gravel	650-555-8734	Rafal Bolinski		
Bowden Steam Plumbing	650-555-3213	Brenda Bowden	06/30/2020	05/31/2020
Brenda's Framing Service	650-555-8888	Brenda	06/30/2020	04/30/2020

As a last step, it is suggested that the report be "memorized" for future use. See Chapter Twelve for details on how to have QuickBooks memorize reports.

Notes:

_____
_____
_____
_____
_____
_____
_____
_____
_____
_____
_____
_____
_____
_____
_____
_____
_____
_____
_____
_____
_____
_____
_____
_____
_____
_____
_____
_____
_____
_____
_____
_____
_____
_____
_____
_____
_____
_____
_____
_____

Chapter Six

Using QuickBooks Payroll for Job Costing

Overview

QuickBooks payroll is a cost effective way for contractors to pay their employees and track job related payroll expenses. QuickBooks payroll has a myriad of functionality, including:

- Prepare weekly, biweekly, monthly, or special run paychecks
- Process hourly and salary paychecks
- Direct deposit or live checks
- Process employee and employer payroll taxes
- Electronic payment of Federal, State, and Local payroll taxes
- Electronic filing of payroll tax returns
- Generate year end W-2s
- Allow for all types of pre- and post-tax employee withholding – voluntary, garnishments, employee loan repayments
- Withholding for 401(k) and employer match accounting
- Track employee vacations and other time off
- Create expense/accrual entries for Workers' Compensation insurance
- Track Workers' Compensation payroll by state and wage class
- Complete posting of transactions to the ledger and job cost
- Create "accruals" of expenses such as general liability insurance
- Generate Certified Payroll reports

This section will focus on functionality that enables the recording of payroll and related expenses to jobs, and reports that allow for management of job related payroll expenses. In order to use the functionality described in this section, a company must have a current Enhanced Payroll subscription from QuickBooks. The following topics will be covered:

- The Preferences and Lists that must be set up to properly job cost payroll
- Using the weekly timesheet to track hours and pay by job
- Setting up QuickBooks to track multi-state workers' compensation payrolls and expense accruals
- Generating Certified Payroll reports for weekly reporting

- Using Company Contribution Payroll Item Codes to track payroll related expenses, such as general liability insurance based on a percentage of payroll
- Dealing with the problem of payroll taxes and other expenses that can only be set up to post to one account

Setting Preferences for Job Cost Payroll and Workers' Comp

Job Costing of payroll and workers' compensation insurance tracking must both be enabled in the Preferences section. From the main menu, select the Edit tab, then Preferences, then Payroll and Employees, then Company Preferences.

Click on the check box for Job Costing and Item tracking for paycheck expenses, as shown below.

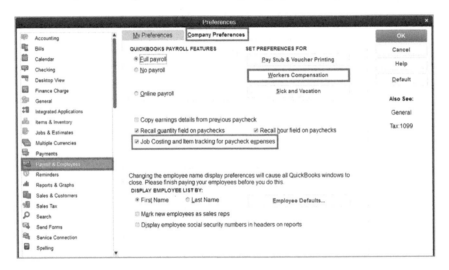

Next, select the Workers' Compensation tab from the above screen and select all of the options as shown below. This assumes that your overtime premium pay is excluded from the calculation of workers' compensation, which is the case for most policies.

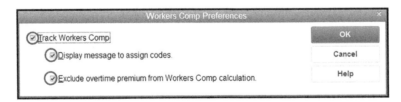

Using The Weekly Timesheet to Track Hours and Pay By Job

The QuickBooks payroll module gives the user the option to record employees time on a weekly timesheet, an ideal method for recording time for field personnel that is to be job costed. The timesheet has inputs for several codes that drive job cost accounting. These codes charge payroll to jobs and item codes within jobs, the rate of pay for which the employee will be paid, and the calculation of workers' compensation. Shown below is a completed timesheet. Note that two jobs are charged with each job assigned a workers' comp code for the respective state.

Workers' Compensation Costing and Management

For many contractors, workers' compensation insurance is a large expense. This insurance is normally calculated as a percentage of payroll, with more hazardous types of labor charged higher percentages. Typically, a company must estimate its payroll by class of labor and by state so that an estimated premium can be determined and paid at the beginning of the policy year. At the end of the policy year, insurance companies audit payroll and either bill for additional premium or provide a credit for overpayment.

QuickBooks can track the details related to multi-state payroll so that managers can determine where they stand with regard to payroll estimates, and make generating the reports needed for payroll audits hassle free. In addition, QuickBooks payroll automatically makes entries based on payroll and workers' comp classes charging jobs the appropriate expense for the categories of work and state.

There are several codes and preferences that must be set up to track workers' compensation:

- Preference for Workers' Comp tracking in Payroll and Employees Preference Area (described above)
- Workers' Comp Payroll Item Code
- Workers' Comp Codes
- Setting the Experience Modification Factor
- Setting Default Workers' Comp codes for employee

Modifying the Workers' Comp Payroll Item Code

Once you've set up your payroll subscription with QuickBooks, this payroll item code is set up automatically. The code may need to be edited so that workers' comp expenses are tracked by job and the entries created are posted to the desired accounts.

To edit the code:

From the main menu, select Lists, then Payroll Item Lists, which will bring up the list as shown below. Click on the Workers' Compensation Code to highlight it, then at the bottom left of the screen, select the down arrow of the Payroll Item tab and the Edit Payroll Item option.

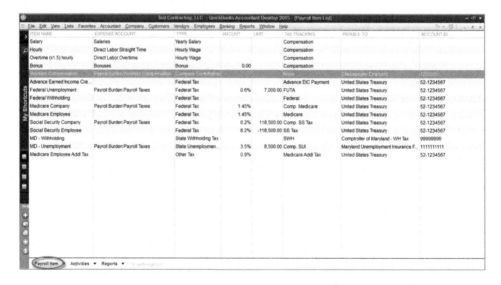

This brings up two screens that allow for edits. In the first screen, be sure to check the option "Track Expenses by Job" so that workers' compensation expense is recorded at the job level.

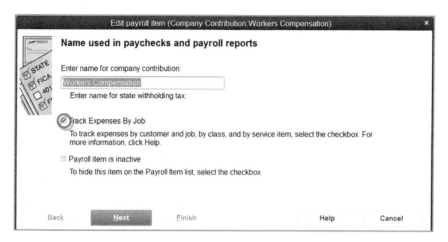

In the second screen, the particulars of your policy can be entered, as well as the accounts to which QuickBooks posts the workers' comp transactions. QuickBooks will post a credit to the Liability account and a debit to the Expense account when recording workers' comp expense.

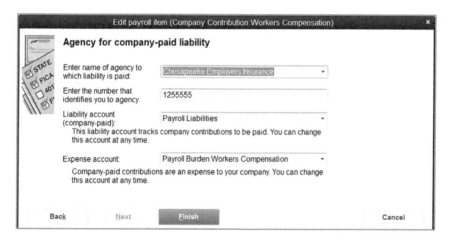

Setting Up Workers' Comp Codes

Once the preference for workers' comp has been turned on, workers' comp codes need to be set up for each class of labor and each state in which the company operates. These rates are found in the company's workers' compensation policy, and are expressed as a percentage of "subject" payroll. When payroll is generated, the associated workers' compensation insurance expense is also calculated by multiplying the payroll dollars for each workers' comp code by its respective rate.

A few pointers:

- In calculating the rates to enter into QuickBooks, make sure to factor in all of the discounts and/ or surcharges that appear in your policy. These items can make a significant difference in the

© The CFO Source, LLC 2015

calculation of your "effective" workers' comp rate. In many cases, the stated rates in the policy multiplied by the estimated payroll does not come close to the total estimated premium.

- QuickBooks provides the option of inputting your experience modification factor, with the default being 100%. It is suggested to use the default rate and incorporate the experience modification into each workers' comp class rate.

To set up workers' compensation rates, begin at the main menu and go to Employees, then drop down to Workers' Compensation, then select Workers' Comp List. This screen will appear:

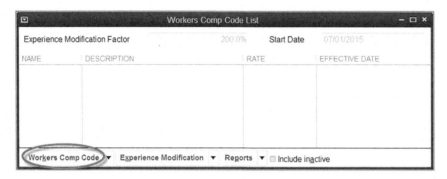

Selecting the drop down arrow on the Workers' Comp Code section will bring up the option of adding a new code. Below is a completed set-up for the masonry class code for Maryland. The codes should be the same codes as are in your policy.

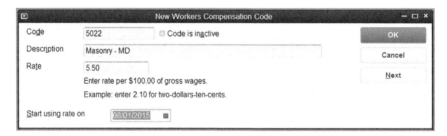

Below is the Workers' Comp Code list completed for a multistate masonry company that has their office payroll in one state. Note that the codes for Virginia and DC have been slightly altered to reflect the different rates for each state.

Setting up the Experience Modification Rate

It is recommended that the experience modification rate in QuickBooks be set to 100% (a rate of 1.0) and that the workers' comp rates be adjusted accordingly as described above. To adjust the rate, in the Workers' Comp Code List, click on the down arrow in the Experience Modification tab, choose edit, and input the rate and effective date desired as shown below. Be aware that the rate cannot be changed retroactively.

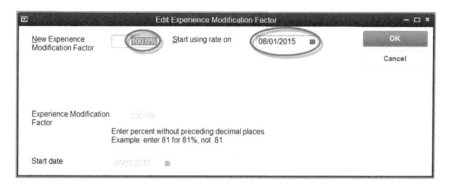

Setting Default Workers' Comp Codes for Employees

QuickBooks gives the user the option of setting default rates for employees. This can be useful for a multi-state company if certain employees only work in one state. To set the default, begin at the main menu and go to Employees, then select the Employee Center, then highlight the employee you wish to set a default rate for. Once the employee has been highlighted, click on the edit icon, as shown circled below.

© The CFO Source, LLC 2015

This will bring up the Edit Employee screen, then select the Workers' Comp tab to select the default rate for the employee using the drop down arrow as shown below.

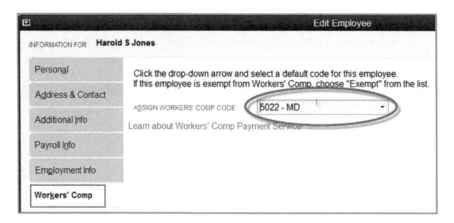

Workers' Compensation Reports

QuickBooks provides several reports that can be used to analyze workers' compensation expenses and make the annual audit go smoothly. These reports are run from the Employees & Payroll section of the Reports menu.

Below is an example of the Workers' Compensation by Code and Employee report, which shows payroll by state and by workers' class code.

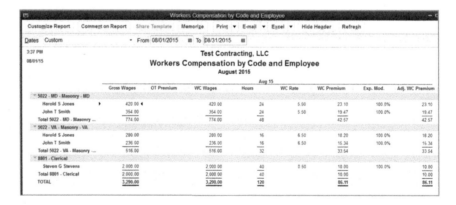

Generating Certified Payroll Reports

For contractors who pay employees for work on jobs subject to "prevailing wages" under the Davis Bacon Act, a weekly report must be submitted to the US Department of Labor, commonly referred to as a "Certified Payroll Report." For contractors using QuickBooks payroll, an Excel add in report comes standard with the QuickBooks Contractors Edition to generate these reports.

From the main menu, select Reports, then Employees & Payroll, then More Reports in Excel, then Certified Payroll Report.

Select Continue to go to the next step.

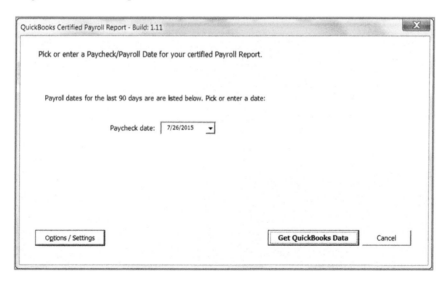

Select the payroll date for which you want to prepare the certified payroll report, and click on Get QuickBooks Data.

At this point a series of interview screens will come up, prompting for the company information that is to appear on the certified payroll report. The first screen is for company name and address:

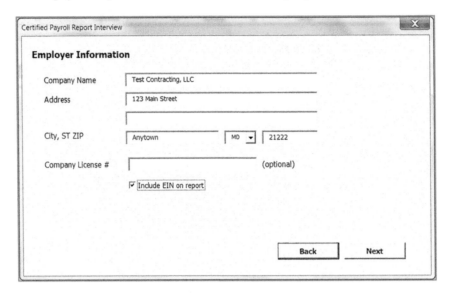

In the next screen the job for which the report is generated can be selected from the drop down shown as "Project Name."

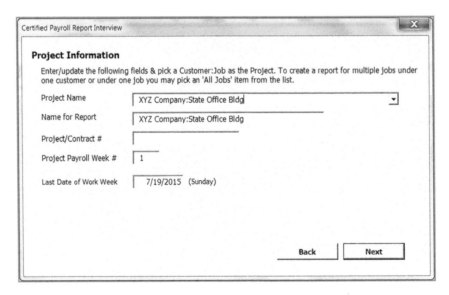

In the last screen before the report is generated, the company official who will be signing the report is designated, as well as whether fringes are to be shown on the report.

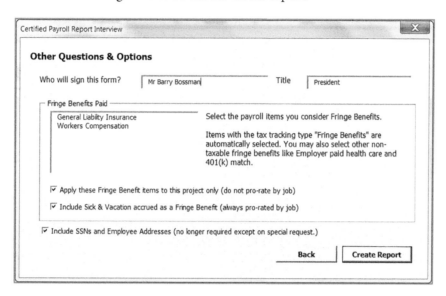

Clicking on Create Report pulls data from QuickBooks into an excel report. As the report is very wide, it will be displayed in two sections. Below is the first section.

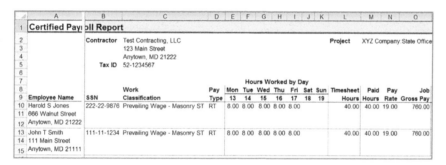

And the second:

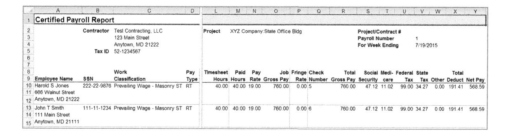

This report should be printed along with the signature page (a separate tab on the excel file) and forwarded to the US Department of Labor.

Using Company Contribution Payroll Item Codes to Charge Non-Payroll Expenses to Jobs

These codes are typically used to record expenses related to employee benefit plans such as 401(k) company matching. However, they can also be set up to generate charges to jobs for items of expense that are related to either payroll hours or dollars. When used in this manner, these codes do not affect employee paychecks and can be set up so that no reference of their use shows to employees. The codes can be used for the following types of transactions:

- General Liability insurance – many of these types of policies are priced as a percentage of "field" payrolls. As such, this cost is purely variable; costs such as these should be included in cost estimates and actual costs charged accordingly.
- Equipment usage – Companies that use large equipment typically estimate the cost of equipment on jobs on the basis of the labor hours they estimate for the equipment operators. For example, an excavating company may want to charge $75.00 per labor hour for the estimated cost of the equipment used on the job.

Below is the process to set up a charge of 4% of field payroll to jobs for general liability insurance expense. Once the code is set up, it is applied to selected employees during the creation of the employee's paycheck. Again, these codes can be set up so that they are transparent to employees, and you'll learn how in the following steps.

To set up a Company Contribution Payroll Item Code:

1. From the main menu, go to Lists.
2. Select Payroll Item List.
3. Select New from the Payroll Item drop down menu at the bottom left. This will bring up the Add New Payroll Item Screen.
4. Select the Custom Setup option (as shown below) and click Next.

5. Select the Company Contribution option, as shown below.

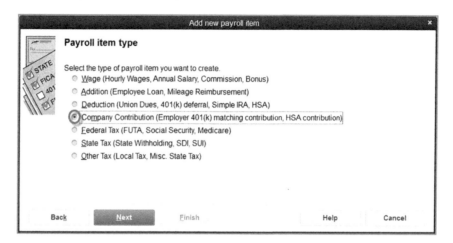

6. Give the payroll item code a name, and make sure to check the Track Expenses by Job option.

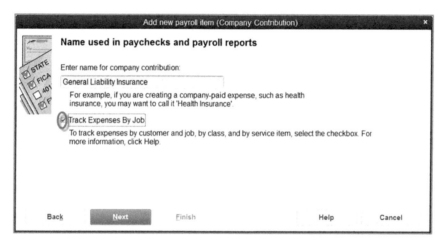

7. Choose the accounts that you want QuickBooks to make the journal entry to. As with the Workers' Comp Item code, QuickBooks will post a credit to the Liability account and a debit to the Expense account when recording transactions with this code.

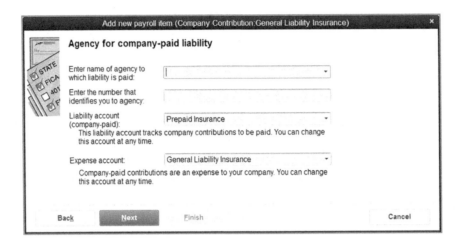

8. Select None for tax tracking.

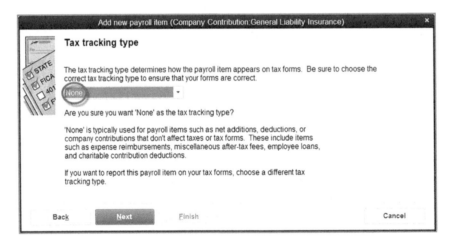

9. Leave all tax options unchecked.

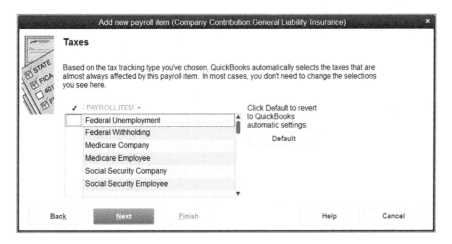

10. If you want the charge to be based on labor hours, select the "Calculate this item based on hours" option. If that is not desired, leave the "Neither" option selected.

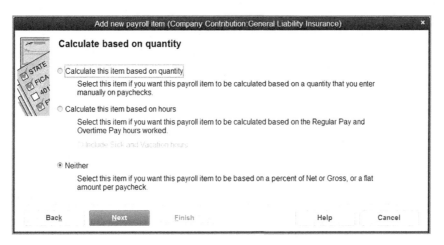

11. The final screen allows the user to select a rate or percentage of payroll for the charge. As shown below, this has been set at 4%.

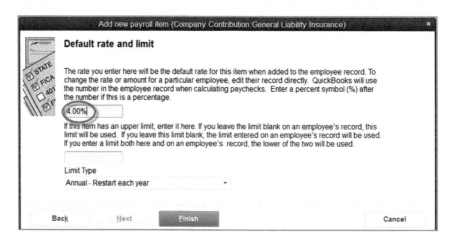

12. Once the item code is set up, the item code should be added to each employee's QuickBooks record so that the charge is automatically generated when processing payroll. The code is added in the Payroll Info tab of an employee's record in the section for Additions, Deductions, and Company Contributions, as shown below.

13. One final step should be taken so that the deduction does not appear on the employee's paycheck. This is done in the Preference section. Go to Payroll and Employees Preferences and select the Pay Stub and Voucher Printing tab as shown below.

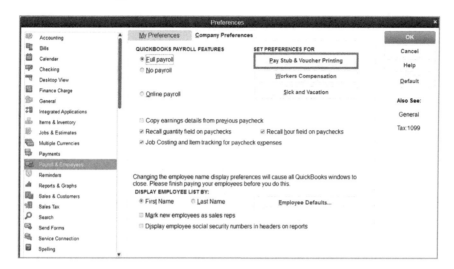

14. Make sure the option to print Non-Taxable Company Items is NOT checked off.

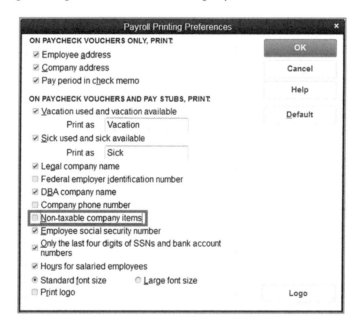

Dealing With the Problem of Payroll Item Codes That Only Post to One Account

A common complaint with QuickBooks payroll is that payroll item codes for payroll taxes and other expenses can only be set up or mapped to one expense account. For example, the employer's portion of social security taxes can only be set up to post to one expense account. The issue is that for financial statement presentation purposes, some companies want to see this expense broken out two ways – the portion related to direct labor categorized in "cost of goods sold" and the portion related to office payrolls categorized in the "expense" area. Two methods to deal with this are available.

Journal Entry Approach

Make a journal entry to reclassify the expense from the account the expenses were posted to, into the desired account. The information would be obtained by running payroll reports for only the employees affected, and making the entry. This, of course, would have to be done on a regular basis.

Company Contribution Payroll Item Code Approach

This approach automates the adjustment and lets QuickBooks payroll make the adjustment every time payroll is generated. The approach uses company contribution payroll item codes in a similar fashion to the cost allocation use described above.

The first step is to set up a company payroll item code that would be assigned only to the employees for which you want to make a reclassification of expenses. For example, if your company had only a few employees for which payroll taxes should be categorized as expense, but a significant number for which payroll taxes should be categorized as cost of goods sold, the new item code would only be assigned to the group in the expense category.

To set up the payroll item code:

1. From the main menu, go to Lists.
2. Select Payroll Item List.
3. At the bottom left, click on the drop down arrow at the Payroll Item tab and select the New option. This will bring up the Add New Payroll Item screen.
4. Choose the Custom Setup option. Click Next.

5. Select the Company Contribution option. Click Next.

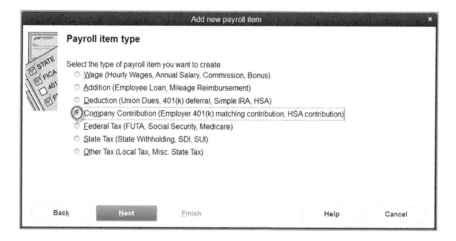

6. Give the payroll item code a name and click on the Track Expenses By Job option. Click Next.

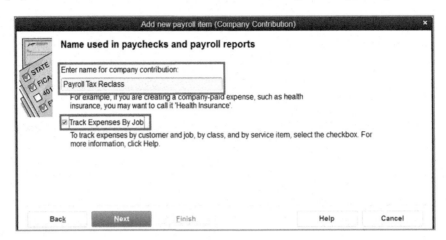

7. The accounts that will be debited and credited when the payroll item code is processed are selected. The Liability Account will receive the credit; in this example, the Cost of Goods Sold account where payroll taxes are originally recorded was selected. The Expense account will receive the debit; in this example, an Expense category account was chosen. In this "work around" neither accounts post to a "Liability" account. Click Next.

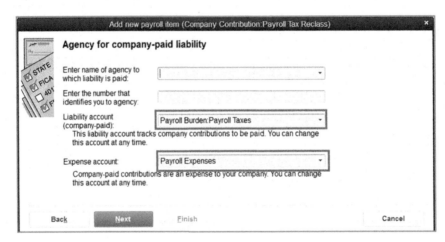

8. The Tax Tracking Type would be selected in the next screen. Because this transaction has no tax implications "None" is selected. Click Next.

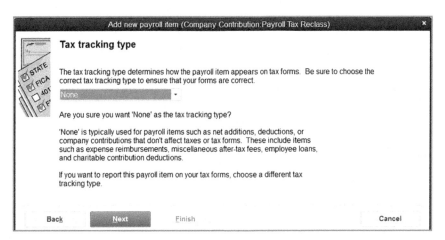

9. Leave all the tax categories unchecked. Click Next.

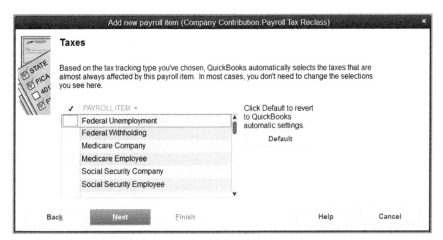

10. Select the neither option. Click Next.

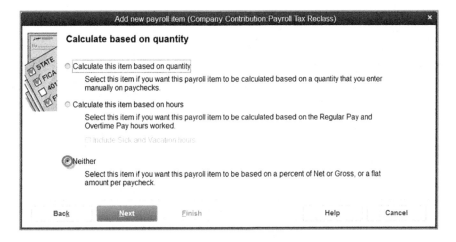

© The CFO Source, LLC 2015

11. Input the percentage that will apply to these transactions. 8% was chosen as an estimate of the FICA rate of 7.65 plus 0.35 for unemployment taxes for this example. Click Finish.

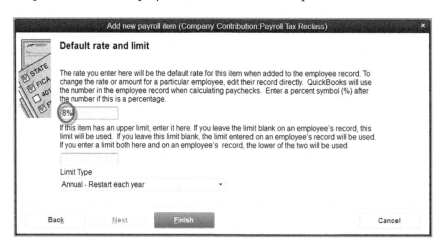

The last step in the process is to assign the new payroll item code to each employee desired. This is done in the Employee Center by editing the payroll tab for an employee. The example below shows the payroll item code assigned to a salaried employee.

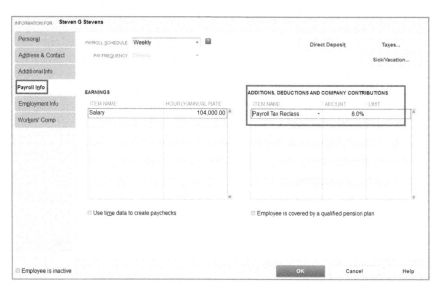

Reclassification done in this manner may not exactly match the actual expenses due to timing differences in areas such as unemployment taxes, but over time, should be fairly accurate.

Notes:

Chapter Seven
Billing for Contracts

Contractors often have billing requirements that are unique to the construction industry. Fortunately, QuickBooks can be set up to handle these requirements so that revenues are recorded properly and receivables tracked for collection. In this section, the following topics will be addressed:

- Two approaches for recording customer prepayments/deposits
- Progress Billing
- Time and Material Billing
- Accounting for retainage billing – jobs in progress and final

Billing for Prepayments/Deposits – Two Approaches

Getting deposits from customers in advance of performing a job is a good business practice. It's a sure sign the customer is committed and good for payment. Two approaches will be presented to handle the accounting for customer deposits.

In the first approach a credit memo is issued to the customer to record the deposit. This approach shows the credit memo as a negative in the customer's receivable record, highlighting that the credit is outstanding and needs to be applied to later billings. While this approach is not technically correct as a customer deposit is really a liability, it has the benefit of keeping the deposit in the receivable area for easy tracking.

The second approach records the deposit in the banking section of QuickBooks. This has the benefit of correctly recording the deposit as a liability, but the deposit will not show in the customer's receivable record, making it something that the user will have to remember outside of QuickBooks.

Approach One - Posting the Deposit to Accounts Receivable with a Credit Memo

This method uses a credit memo to record the deposit (cash receipt) from the customer. A credit memo is issued to the customer such that a debit to cash is created and an offsetting credit recorded to accounts receivable. The credit memo can be printed and given to the customer as a receipt for the payment. The credit on the customer's account can be used later to apply against billings so that invoices to the customer reflect the deposit paid.

The first step is to set up a service item code that maps to the bank account in which the customer prepayment will be deposited.

The item code should be set up as shown below:

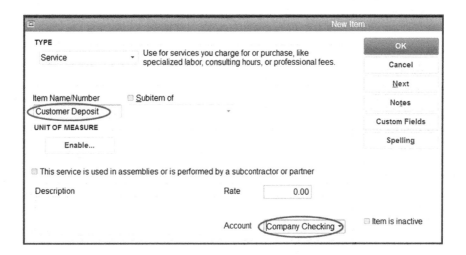

It's suggested that the description field in the credit memo item code be left blank so that the particulars of the transaction can be customized for individual credit memos as they are used. To generate a credit memo, begin at the main menu and go to Customers, then Create Credit Memos/Refunds.

Below is a completed credit memo for a $10,000 deposit.

© The CFO Source, LLC 2015

The credit memo above records an increase in cash and sets up a credit to the customer's account in accounts receivable, as shown below.

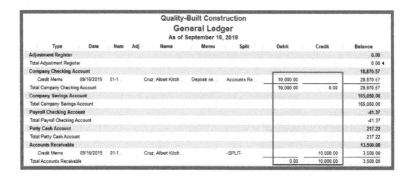

When it comes time to invoice the customer for the project, the customer billing screen allows you to record the full amount of the invoice and apply the credit already issued, which produces an invoice net of the credit. To issue the invoice and apply the credit, begin on the main menu and go to Customers, then Create Invoices, and select the customer/job that you wish to invoice.

Below is an invoice issued to the customer before application of the credit.

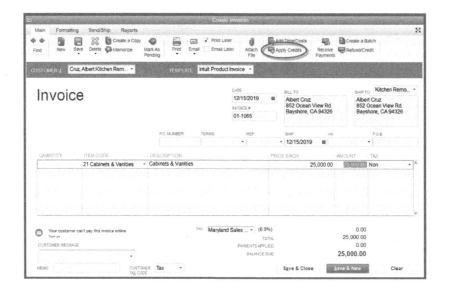

Clicking on the apply credits tab brings up a screen that allows the user to select the appropriate credit to apply, as shown below.

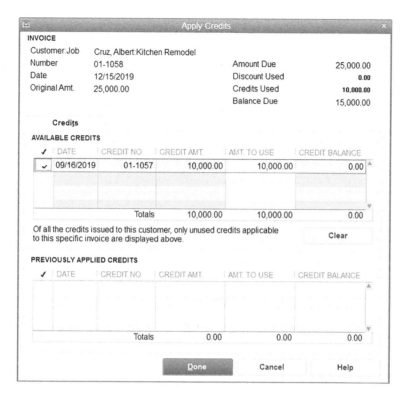

The final invoice is shown below. Note that the credit has been applied to the invoice amount and the net amount due is shown.

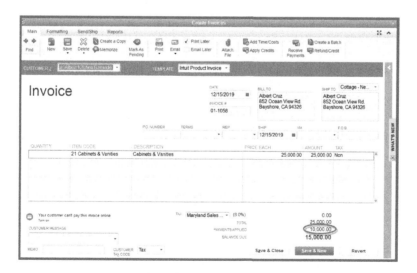

Accounting Comment on this Approach

It is important to realize that a deposit is not revenue when received, but rather a liability of the company which is settled when the services or goods paid for in advance are delivered. Under generally accepted accounting principles, revenue should not be recognized until the work has been performed. The first approach as outlined above takes care of this by not recording the deposit as revenue until an invoice is issued against which the credit memo is applied. However, the credit is recorded as a reduction in Accounts Receivable instead of set up as a Current Liability. In many cases, these amounts are not "material" to the financial statements, and the presentation of these credits as a reduction in the Accounts Receivable account is acceptable. In the event these amounts are significant, a journal entry could be made to transfer the credit balance in Accounts Receivable to a Deposit Payable current liability account, as follows:

	Debit	Credit
Accounts Receivable	$10,000	
Deposits Payable		$10,000

Approach Two - Posting the Deposit to a Current Liability Account

This approach records the cash receipt received at the beginning of the project as a current liability instead of a reduction in Accounts Receivable. As a final step, the deposit is shown on the customer's invoice as a negative amount, with a separate item code mapped to a deposits payable account (a current liability).

The first step is to set up a "Deposits due Customers" account as an Other Current Liability account.

1. Begin at the main menu and go to Lists.
2. Select Chart of Accounts.
3. Click on the drop down arrow in the bottom left corner tab labeled Account.
4. Select the New option.

Below is the set-up for the new account.

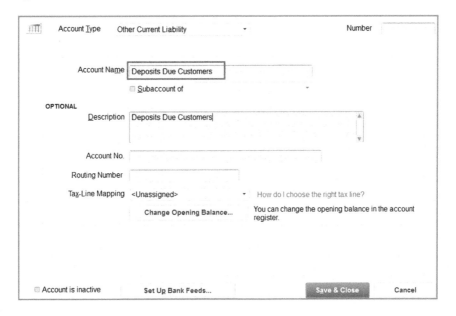

Once the account is set up, record the cash receipt.

1. From the main menu, select Banking.
2. Select Make Deposits.
3. Select the correct bank account and input the Customer:Job the deposit is for.
4. Choose Deposits Due Customers account as the From Account and input the amount as shown below.

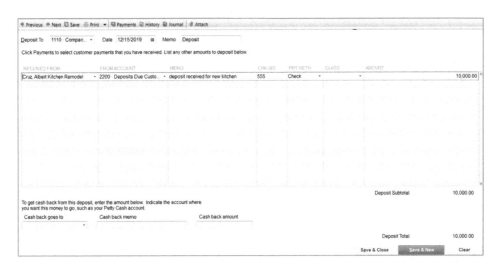

Billing for the job will need to be net of the deposit. In this approach, make the account the Customer Deposits item code maps to the new account set-up, Deposits Due Customers, instead of the cash account.

Below is the change:

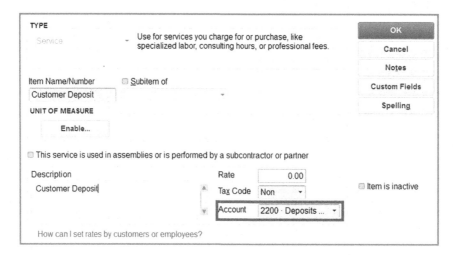

In the billing to the customer, use the Customer Deposit item code as a separate line item with a negative amount to reduce the bill to the desired net amount as shown below.

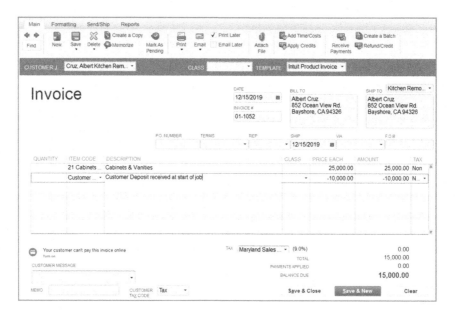

Here's the general ledger detail showing the initial recording of the deposit as a cash receipt and subsequent application to the total invoice, leaving a zero balance.

Progress Billing

Contractors are often required to submit progress billings based on predetermined percentages in the contracts with their customers. For example, a contractor may bill for 10% of the contract value at mobilization, another 50% at a certain milestone, and the final 40% upon completion. QuickBooks has built in functionality that will do progress billing provided an estimate for the job is set up under Customer and Job. In addition, the preference for progress billing must be turned on in the Jobs and Estimates section as shown below.

There are three options available for progress billing:

- Create invoice for the entire estimate (100%)
- Create invoice for a percentage of the entire estimate
- Create invoice for selected items, for different percentages of each item

Choosing the third option may result in certain items not being billed in the progress invoice being prepared. Unbilled items will appear on the invoice as zeroes unless the preference "Don't print items that have zero amount" is checked.

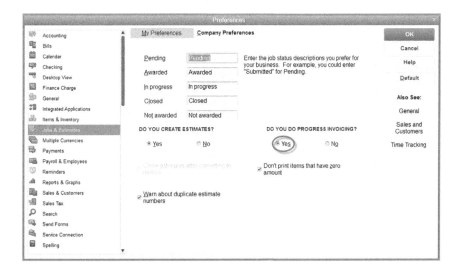

© The CFO Source, LLC 2015

Below is an example that will be used to demonstrate QuickBooks progress billing.

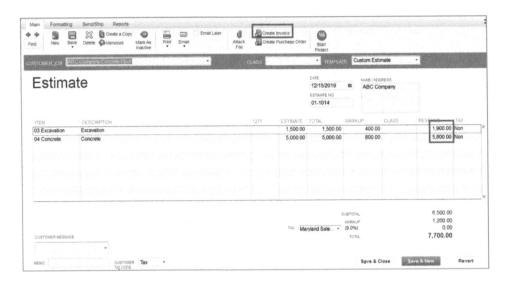

In the example above, there are two items that make up the estimate, adding to a total contract value of $7,700.00. Progress billing can be applied separately to each line on the estimate. To create a progress invoice, while in the estimate screen for the job, click on the Create Invoice tab, which will bring up the Create Progress Invoice Based on Estimate screen. In the example below, the option to create an invoice for selected items or for different percentages of each item was selected.

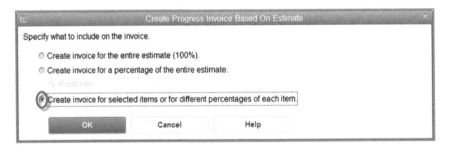

Selecting this option brings up the screen where you can enter the amount of the progress billing you wish to create. The billing can be based on quantities or percentages. In the below example, 100% of the first item and 50% of the second will be billed.

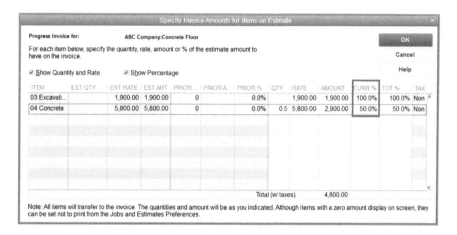

Below is an example of the progress invoice.

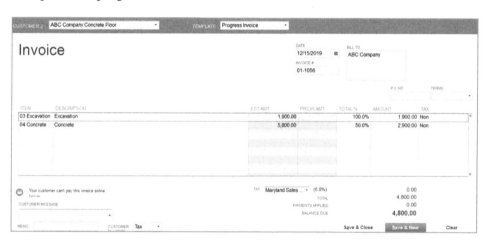

When billing for additional amounts under the estimate, QuickBooks will also show the prior amount billed on the invoice (in the EST AMT column) and will not let you create an invoice for more than 100% of the estimate.

Time and Material Billing

Some contracts call for the billing of costs incurred with agreed upon markup or unit cost, typically known as time and material contracts. QuickBooks has the functionality in the billing module to "call up" costs and time charged to a job and post those costs to a customer invoice. From there, markup can be added and the bill issued.

To enable this functionality, it must be turned on in the Preferences section.

1. From the main menu, select Edit.
2. Select Preferences.
3. Select Time & Expenses.
4. In the Company tab of this preference, check off all of the time tracking and invoicing options as shown below. If you have a standard markup, make that your default percentage.

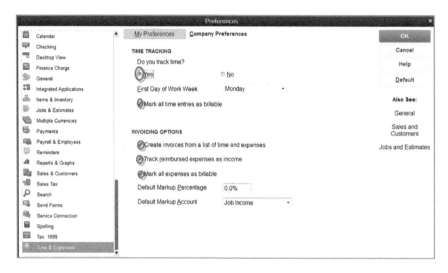

QuickBooks has a separate billing option in the customer section for creating invoices for Time and Expenses. This option allows the user to select from four areas of cost in the creation of an invoice. These are Time, Expenses, Mileage, and Items. It's important to understand how costs in each of the four categories are recorded and transferred to time and material invoices so that customer invoices are prepared as desired.

When time and material billing is created, accounts receivable is debited at the customer level, while the offsetting credit(s) is determined based on how the underlying vendor cost was created. Additionally, the descriptions that appear on Time and Material billing are dependent on how the underlying costs are generated. Each area will be reviewed below.

Time

The hours used for Time billings originate in the payroll area, using the hours charged to jobs recorded as part of preparing payroll.

The rate charged, account credited, and description used for Time billings are based on the Sales Information section of the item code used for the payroll charge. Below is a sample for a Masonry Charge.

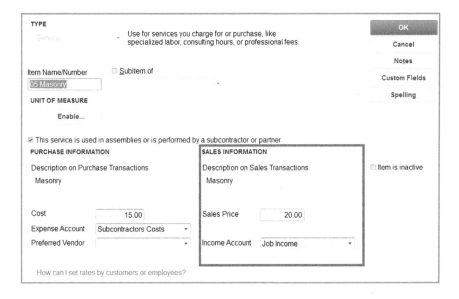

Expenses

This area of cost originates when a vendor bill is processed using the Expenses tab and is assigned to a job.

For vendor bills processed using the Expenses tab, the QuickBooks default setting is to have billing credits posted to the originating expense account. The effect of this is to zero out the expense. If it is desired to have the billing credit posted to an income account, the account must be edited to indicate the account to be credited. Below is an account edited to post billing credits to a different account.

© The CFO Source, LLC 2015

A few key points:

- Any Income Account assigned to an Expense Account can only be used once. In the above example, Job Income, once assigned to the Insurance Expense account cannot be assigned to another expense account.
- If multiple expense accounts are to be used in this fashion, then multiple Income accounts would need to be set up. A parent/sub account set-up is recommended if this is the case. For financial statement presentation purposes, the sub accounts could be hidden so that only the total is shown.
- The mapping for bill credits is not available for Cost of Goods Sold accounts. Note, in the below account set-up for a Cost of Goods Sold account, the mapping option is not there.

For vendor bills processed with the Expense tab, an explanation for the charge must be input into the memo line on the bill so that an explanation for the bill will be transferred to the Time and Material invoice. Shown below is a properly completed bill. Make sure to input the Customer:Job information and that the billable box is checked.

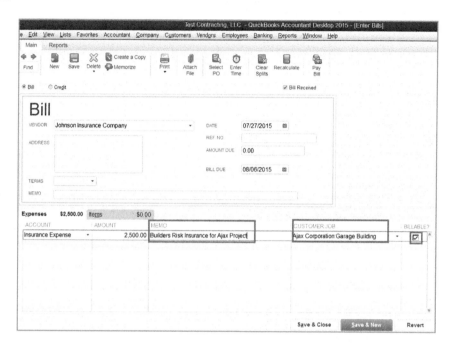

Mileage

The amounts transferred to Time and Material billing for mileage originate when vehicle mileage is recorded in the Enter Vehicle Mileage screen.

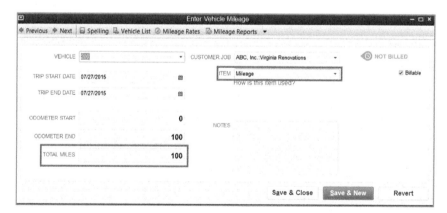

The amount of mileage transferred is based on the miles entered, multiplied by the Sales Price of the item used to record the mileage. As shown below, a separate Mileage Item code has been set up with a Sales Price of $0.60.

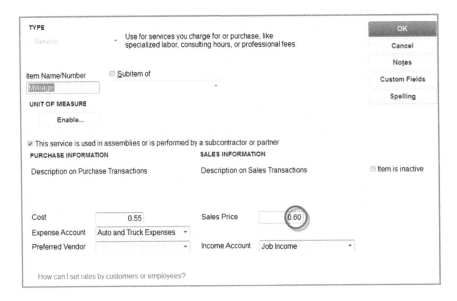

Items

This area of cost originates when a vendor bill is processed using the Items tab and is assigned to a job.

The account credited and description used for vendor bills processed using the Items tab is based on the Sales Information section of the item code used for the payroll charge. The amount transferred to the Time and Materials billing is based on the quantities entered on the vendor invoice, multiplied by the Sales Price set up for the item code. If no quantity is entered, a quantity of one will be assigned.

For vendor bills recorded using the Items tab, the offsetting credit will be made to the Income Account shown in the Sales Information of the item code set up. The item code shown below is set to have the credits posted to the Job Income account.

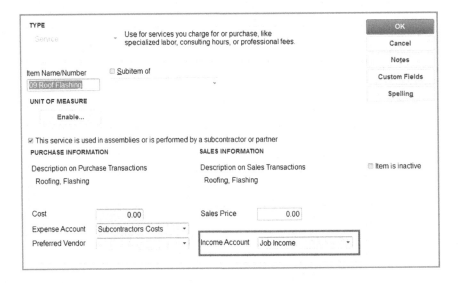

For vendor costs recorded with the Items tab, the Item Description carries over in Time and Material billing. As shown below, the wording in the Description on Sales Transactions area is what will carry over.

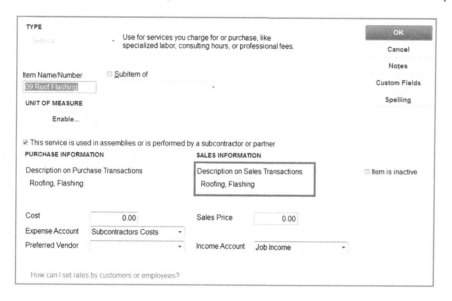

Generating a Time and Material Invoice

To generate a time and material invoice to a customer:

1. From the main menu, select Customers.
2. Select Invoice for Time and Expenses. This will bring up the Invoice for Time & Expenses screen where you can select the job you want to bill, the date range of expense transactions to include, and whether you want to select specific billable items.

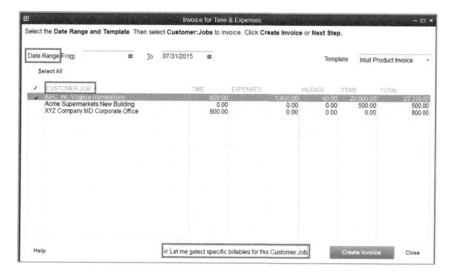

After selecting a job and clicking on the Create Invoice tab, the Choose Billable Time and Costs screen will appear, allowing the user to tab through all four areas and select the transactions that are to be billed. Below is the screen for the selection of Time charges to include on the bill.

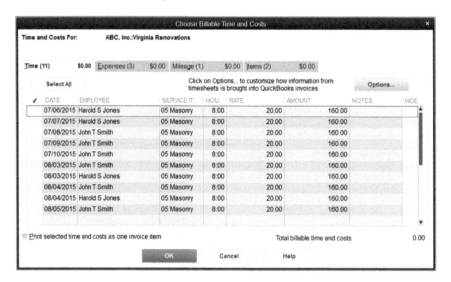

Selecting the Options tab will bring up the following screen, which lets the user specify the level of detail to be shown on the invoice.

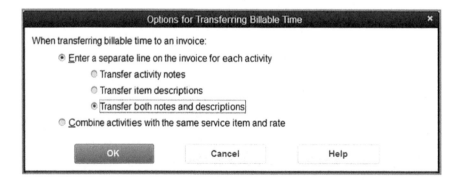

In the Expenses tab, in addition to selecting the costs to bill, the user can select the desired markup for this portion of the bill and the account to which the markup will be credited. Keep in mind, the credit for the cost part of this billing is driven by the account set-up, with the default being a credit to the originating expense.

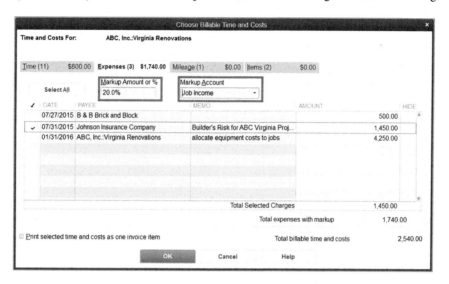

In the Mileage tab, the user can select mileage to be invoiced. The options tab in this section provides the same options as in the Time tab.

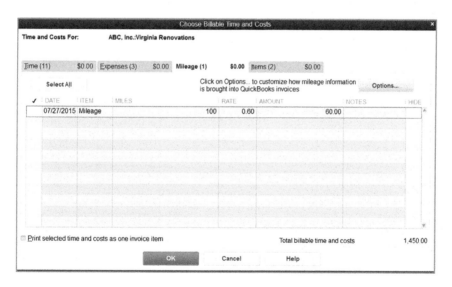

In the Items tab, the desired items are selected to appear on the bill.

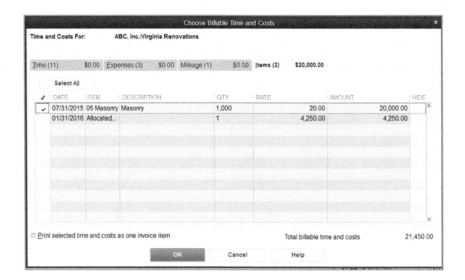

Below is the body of the invoice generated.

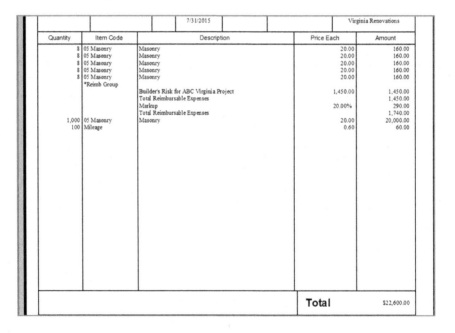

Alternative Approach to Time and Material Billing

QuickBooks Time and Material billing has numerous set-up requirements, and in some cases, the billing amounts generated are more "price" billing than "cost plus" billing.

If true "cost plus" billing is required, a profit and loss statement for the job to be billed could be generated and the detailed cost transactions exported to Excel for further formatting.

Retention Billing

Retention is the practice of owners or general contractors holding back or "retaining" a percentage (typically 10%) of the amount of progress billings while construction is under way. Payment of the amounts withheld under retention billing is typically made upon completion of construction. QuickBooks can be set up to record the reduction from progress billings for the amounts to be retained, as well as to prepare a final bill at the end of the project for the entire amounts withheld.

A Retentions Receivable account should be set up to track retention using the account type of Other Current Asset.

1. From the main menu, go to Lists.
2. Choose Chart of Accounts.
3. At the bottom left, click on Account.
4. Choose New from the drop down menu.

Below is the completed set-up.

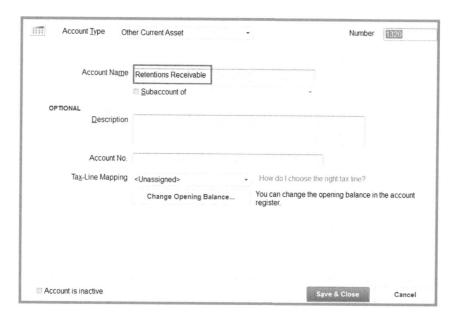

© The CFO Source, LLC 2015

A retention item code must also be set up, which will be used on the customer invoice. In the below Item code set-up screen, the Retention item code maps to the Retention Other Asset Account. Also note that the amount has been set to a minus 10%, which will serve to create a reduction in the customer invoice.

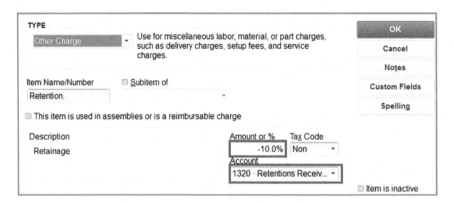

Deducting retention from an invoice involves first creating a subtotal of the items, then applying the 10% retention deduction from the subtotal. If not all items on an invoice are subject to a retention deduction, these should be placed below the retention line. Below is the previous progress billing with retention applied.

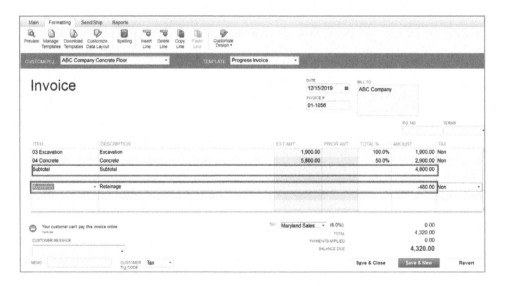

Because retention is tracked in an Other Current Asset account and not an Accounts Receivable account, the amount of retention deducted from progress billings cannot be shown by running customer accounts receivable aging reports. However, these retention deductions can be shown by running either the Customer Balance Summary or Detail report and filtering the report for the Retentions Receivable account.

Below is the Detail report from a sample company; note that the last customer's balance is zero due to the billing at the end of the job for all of the retention deductions on progress billings.

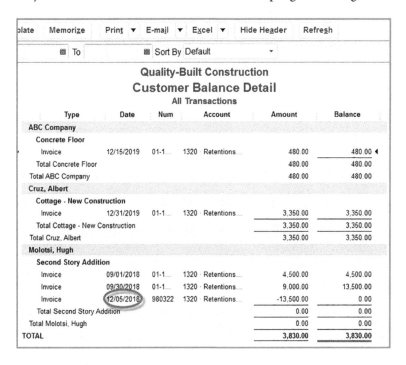

A final retention invoice must be created to clear out the balance in the retention receivable account and transfer the balance to the regular accounts receivable account so that payment when received can be applied. An invoice for final retention is shown below.

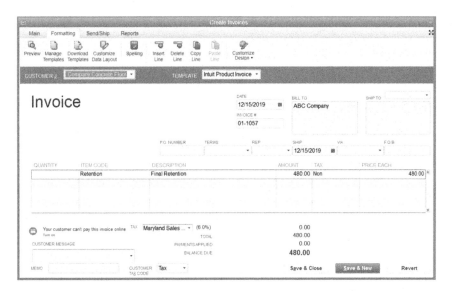

© The CFO Source, LLC 2015

Below are the transactions in the Retention Receivable account for the example shown above.

Notes:

Chapter Eight

Equipment and Vehicle Costing

Equipment and vehicle expenses are a large part of the cost structure for many contractors. Knowing what these costs are and developing a way to incorporate these costs into job estimates and allocate costs to jobs is critical. This section will look at two major areas:

- Setting up QuickBooks to track equipment and vehicle costs
- Methods for allocating costs to jobs

Set-Up

The Chart of Accounts can be customized to track vehicle and equipment expenses, and provide detail at the individual asset level while also providing useful fleet totals. By using three levels of accounts a complete picture of these costs can be developed. Additionally, by using separate accounts to allocate costs to jobs it can be determined if costs are over or under allocated.

The first step is to set up two accounts:

1. Job Equipment Costs – this should be a Cost of Goods Sold account type. This account will be charged cost at the Customer:Job level as allocations of cost. No actual equipment cost such as fuel, maintenance, etc. should be charged to this account.
2. Equipment Costs – this should be an Expenses account type. This account will serve to total all equipment costs and will have numerous sub and sub-sub accounts.

The second step is to set up sub accounts and sub-sub accounts under the Equipment Costs account. These accounts should be set up with an account type of Expenses. These are as follows:

Sub-Account	Sub-Sub-Accounts
Equipment Rentals	None
Fuel	None
Licenses	None
Insurance	None
Depreciation	None
Repairs and Maintenance	One for each piece of equipment, vehicle, etc.
Equipment Costs Allocated to Jobs	None

Comments:

- The Equipment Rentals account should be used for equipment rented or leased on an ongoing basis and used for multiple jobs. A separate Cost of Goods Sold account should be set up for rentals specific to individual jobs.
- All of the sub and sub-sub accounts, except the Equipment Costs Allocated to Jobs account, are the accounts to which actual expenses are to be charged.
- The Equipment Costs Allocated to Job account will receive a credit as part of the allocation with the debit going to the Cost of Goods Sold account Job Equipment Costs. No actual expense should be charged to either of these accounts.

Below is a sample section of a P & L set-up with an allocation of equipment costs as an expense.

Test Contracting, LLC
Profit & Loss
January 2016

	Jan 16
▾ Ordinary Income/Expense	
▾ Cost of Goods Sold	
Job Equipment Cost	10,750.00
Total COGS	10,750.00 ◄
Gross Profit	-10,750.00
▾ Expense	
Eqp Costs Allocated to Jobs	10,750.00
▾ Equipment Costs	
Depreciation	750.00
Equipment Rentals	1,200.00
Fuel	2,755.55
Insurance	1,200.00
Licenses	275.55
▾ Repairs and Maintenance	
2014 F350 Pickup	2,250.00
Cat Bulldozer	1,745.45
Cat Grader	625.00
New Holland Skid Loader	352.00
Total Repairs and Maintenance	4,972.45
Total Equipment Costs	11,153.55
Total Expense	403.55
Net Ordinary Income	-11,153.55
Net Income	-11,153.55

Note that the allocation of $10,750 of equipment cost serves to increase Cost of Goods Sold while decreasing Total Expenses. Actual Total Equipment Costs are shown as $11,153.55, indicating that the allocation of $10,750 left $403.55 unallocated. Tracking of the over or under allocated amount over time will give a good indication of the accuracy of the allocation formula.

Allocating Costs to Jobs

Two methods to allocate costs to jobs will be presented. The selection of the method is based on whether it is desired to track expenses at the item code level so that the Job Estimates vs. Actuals reports can be used. If this reporting is not desired, the allocation can be done with a journal entry. If the reporting is desired, the allocation should be done via the Enter Bills approach.

In either approach, some basis for the allocation will need to be determined. For example, charging jobs based on an equipment cost per field labor hours is a reasonable approach. In some cases, only labor hours of equipment operators may be appropriate. It is strongly suggested that accountants discuss the approach taken with estimators so that an approach best fitting for your company can be developed.

In the journal entry approach, debits to the Job Equipment Cost account are made at the job level with the offsetting credit to the Equipment Costs Allocated to Jobs account. Below is a sample of the entry. Note that it is not necessary to use a job code on the credit side of the transaction.

The second approach is referred to as the "Enter Bills" approach, as the allocation is recorded as a bill in the Vendor section of QuickBooks. In this approach, a zero-dollar vendor bill is recorded with 1) charges made to an item code that maps to the Cost of Goods Sold account "Job Equipment Costs" and one entry for each job to be charged, and 2) a negative Expense is recorded to the Eqp Costs Allocated to Jobs account. The net of the bill must be zero.

To implement the Enter Bills approach, first set up a dummy vendor under which to record the bill. In the example below, we've create a vendor called "Allocation Vendor."

The next step is to create a service item code that maps to the Cost of Goods Sold account Job Equipment Costs. Below is the set-up for the new code.

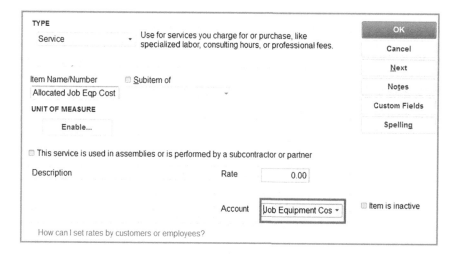

After setting up the item code, you can record the transaction. This can be done by selecting Vendors from the main menu, then Enter Bills. There are two steps to record the transaction. The first step is in the Items tab of the Enter Bills screen, where each job to be charged is entered on a separate line as shown below.

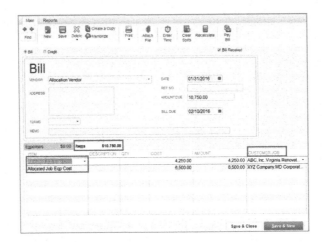

The second step is done in the Expenses tab, where only the total of the allocations is entered as a negative, serving to "zero out" the transaction. Below is the Expenses tab part of the transaction. Note: no job information is needed in the Expenses tab part of the transaction.

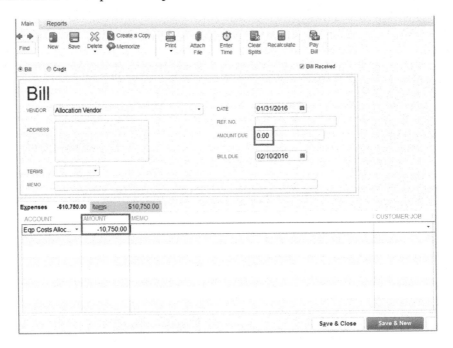

The transaction journal below shows the accounting QuickBooks does for the transaction. The net effect to accounts payable is zero, while the charges to jobs are done at the item code level.

nent on Report   Share Template   Memorize   Print ▾   E-mail ▾   Excel ▾   Hide Header   Refresh

From   To   Sort By Default

Test Contracting, LLC
Transaction Journal
All Transactions

Trans #	Type	Date	Num	Name	Item	Account	Debit	Credit
11	Bill	01/31/2016		Allocation Vendor		Accounts Payable	0.00	
				Allocation Vendor		Eqp Costs Allocated to Jobs		10,750.00
				ABC, Inc.:Virginia...	Allocated Job Eqp Cost	Job Equipment Cost	4,250.00	
				XYZ Company:MD...	Allocated Job Eqp Cost	Job Equipment Cost	6,500.00	
							10,750.00	10,750.00
TOTAL							10,750.00	10,750.00

Notes:

_____

_____

_____

_____

_____

_____

_____

_____

_____

_____

_____

_____

_____

_____

_____

_____

_____

_____

_____

_____

_____

_____

_____

_____

_____

_____

_____

_____

_____

_____

_____

_____

_____

_____

_____

_____

_____

_____

Chapter Nine

Inventory Costing

Overview

Some contractors stock large quantities of standard materials that are used on many of their jobs, taking advantage of quantity discounts for these purchases. These contractors will want to be able to charge jobs for material usage and track the quantities of inventory on hand. The inventory functionality in QuickBooks can be set up to handle this.

It's important to understand how inventory in QuickBooks is designed, as it is not meant for a materials inventory but can easily be adapted. QuickBooks inventory is designed for companies in the business of buying inventory for resale, where a price and cost per item is set up. Typically, the price for an item is input as part of the invoicing process, while cost for an item is driven by the recording of vendor bills.

In the QuickBooks inventory module, each sale of an item creates two transactions in QuickBooks:

- Revenue is recorded with an offsetting accounts receivable and
- Cost of the goods is recognized along with a reduction in inventory.

The second transaction happens automatically, triggered by quantities invoiced to customers and the unit costs that were previously input.

Many contractors, however, do not bill customers for labor and materials separately, but rather combine all phases of a job into one line item. By billing a zero dollar invoice to the Customer:Job with the quantities desired, the cost of goods sold transaction and accompanying reduction in inventory transaction will occur with no effect to income or accounts receivable.

Setting Up and Using Inventory

The first step in setting up QuickBooks for inventory is to turn on the Preference for inventory.

1. From the main menu, select Edit.
2. Select Preferences.

3. Select Items and Inventory.
4. In the Company Preferences tab, check the "Inventory and purchase orders are active." box as shown below.

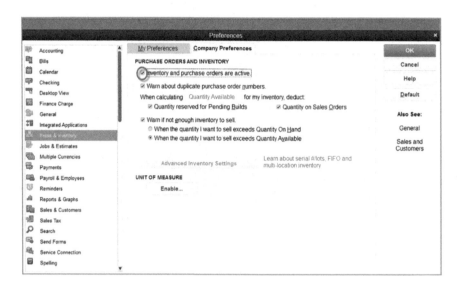

Next, make sure that a materials account is set up on your Chart of Accounts. For most contractors, this should be a Cost of Goods Sold account.

Inventory transactions require that Inventory Part item codes be set up. As with other item codes, these can be set up with Parent and sub items to fit your needs. Below is a set-up for a masonry contractor using 12" Block.

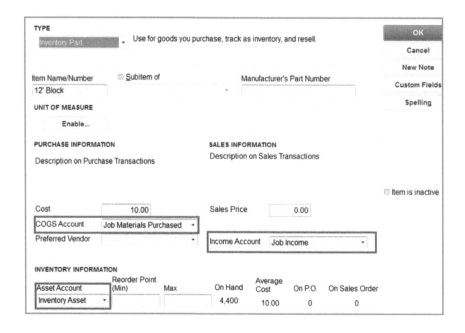

A few important notes:

- The Cost of Goods Sold account is where the expense for materials will be charged.
- The Inventory Asset account is where purchases processed with this item code will be charged and where the usage will be deducted.
- The Income account is a required field, and zero-dollar transactions will appear in this account. Note: the sales price is zero.

To record purchases of materials for inventory:

- From the main menu, select Vendors.
- Select Enter Bills.
- Using the Items tab, select the desired item code(s), then input your quantity and unit price.

Below is a completed bill for a masonry vendor's purchase of block. The unit cost of the material is $10.00. This unit cost will be used later when the material is charged to a job. A Customer:Job number is not required on the bill as the materials are being purchased for inventory, not for a specific job.

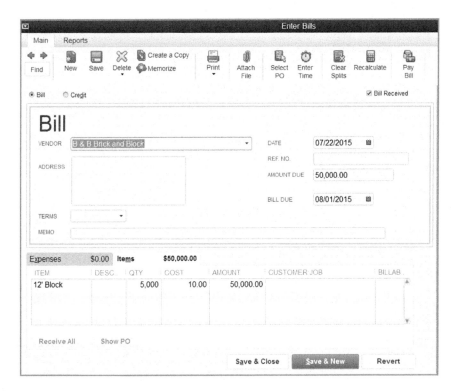

© The CFO Source, LLC 2015

To charge a job for the use of inventory, a zero-dollar invoice for the item(s) used is created. Below is the invoice for a job using the block shown as purchased above. Quantities are shown with a price of zero and the invoice is marked as paid.

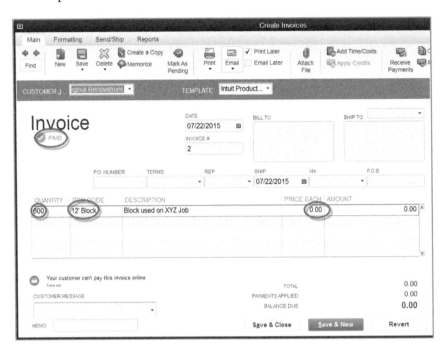

Below is a custom report showing only the accounts affected by the purchase of inventory and zero-dollar billing in the example above. The bill from B&B Block increased accounts payable and inventory, while the zero-dollar invoice only serves to reduce inventory and recognize the cost of goods sold. There is no effect to income or accounts receivable.

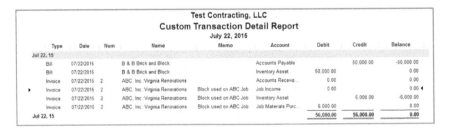

Also available to the contractor when using this approach, is the myriad of reports on inventory usage and balances. For example, below is a report showing the activity in the inventory item code used in the example above.

Test Contracting, LLC
Inventory Valuation Detail
July 1 - 22, 2015

	Type	Date	Name	Num	Qty	Cost	On Hand	Avg Cost	Asset Value
Inventory									
12' Block									
	Bill	07/22/2015	B & B Brick and Block		5.000	50,000.00	5.000	10.00	50,000.00
	Invoice	07/22/2015	ABC, Inc.:Virginia Renovations	2	-600		4,400	10.00	44,000.00 ◄
Total 12' Block							4,400		44,000.00
Total Inventory							4,400		44,000.00
TOTAL							4,400		44,000.00

Making Inventory Adjustments

A good management practice is to take periodic physical inventories of materials and compare actual quantities on hand with the balances showing in QuickBooks. Adjustments can be made so that QuickBooks matches the physical count. This is done in the Vendor section.

1. From the main menu, select Vendors.
2. Select Inventory Activities.
3. Select Adjust Quantities/Values.

There are three options when making adjustments – Quantities Total Value, or both Quantities and Value. Shown below is the adjustment screen.

Adjustments can be made to post to the same account as inventory usage is charged or another account can be selected. Only one job can be charged at a time, if it is desired to spread inventory adjustments over several jobs, multiple smaller adjustments would be recommended.

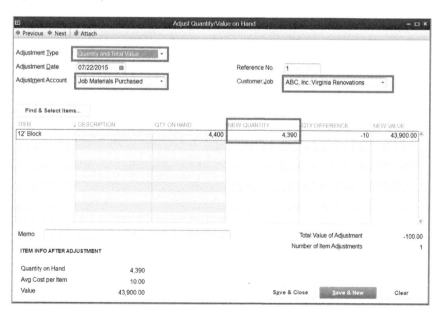

© The CFO Source, LLC 2015

Inventory adjustments will show on reports as unique transaction types, as shown in the below Inventory Valuation Detail Report.

Test Contracting, LLC
Inventory Valuation Detail
July 1 - 25, 2015

Type	Date	Name	Num	Qty	Cost	On Hand	Avg Cost	Asset Value
Inventory								
12' Block								
Bill	07/22/2015	B & B Bri...		5,000	50,000.00	5,000	10.00	50,000.00
Invoice	07/22/2015	ABC, Inc....	2	-600		4,400	10.00	44,000.00
Inventory Adjust	07/22/2015	ABC, Inc....	1	-10		4,390	10.00	43,900.00
Total 12' Block						4,390		43,900.00
Total Inventory						4,390		43,900.00
TOTAL						4,390		**43,900.00**

Notes:

Chapter Ten
Percentage Completion Accounting

In most situations, generally accepted accounting principles require that the percentage completion method be used to recognize revenue on long term construction projects. Under this method, billings to customers are adjusted to reflect the revenue "earned" per the percentage of completion calculated. The calculation is as follows:

Percentage Complete = Expenses Incurred to Date/Total Estimated Costs

Revenue Earned = Total Contract Value X Percentage Complete

It is critical that the total estimated cost figure is accurate, and best practice is a regular review of the cost estimate as jobs progress. Typically, as jobs progress, a "cost to complete" is calculated, which factors costs incurred to date and estimated costs for the parts of the job that have not been completed.

Banks and surety companies also require that construction companies provide them with detailed schedules of information on contract values, billings, cost estimates, and costs incurred to date. The ability to track and provide this information in a timely and accurate manner is a sign of a well-run contracting company.

QuickBooks *does not* have a module that provides percentage completion reporting with all the required calculations and posting of adjustments to the ledgers. However, the basic information required to prepare a percentage completion schedule can be derived from QuickBooks. In this section, an approach is outlined to get the basic information from QuickBooks, export it to Excel, and generate the needed reporting. This approach is dependent on having both the estimate and actual information up to date in QuickBooks.

The Job Estimate vs. Actual Summary report contains much of the information needed to create a percentage of completion report. To run the report:

1. From the main menu, select Reports.
2. Select Jobs, Time & Mileage, then Job Estimate vs. Actuals Summary.
3. The report should be run through the date for which the percentage completion adjustment is being prepared.

Below is the report showing the columns of data that will be transferred to the percentage completion report you will build in excel.

Test Contracting, LLC Job Estimates vs. Actuals Summary As of August 31, 2015						
	Est. Cost	Act. Cost	($) Diff.	Est. Revenue	Act. Revenue	($) Diff.
ABC, Inc.						
Virginia Renovat...	30,500.00	19,747.09	-10,752.91	42,200.00	27,600.00	-14,600.00
Total ABC, Inc.	30,500.00	19,747.09	-10,752.91	42,200.00	27,600.00	-14,600.00
XYZ Company						
MD Corporate Of...	43,000.00	14,769.95	-28,230.05	57,416.67	10,000.00	-47,416.67
Total XYZ Company	43,000.00	14,769.95	-28,230.05	57,416.67	10,000.00	-47,416.67
TOTAL	73,500.00 ▶	34,517.04 ◀	-38,982.96	99,616.67	37,600.00	-62,016.67

After running the report, it can be exported to Excel and the needed information transferred (copied and pasted from the exported excel document) to a spreadsheet set up for percentage of completion accounting. Below is a completed schedule after export and transfer of the data from QuickBooks.

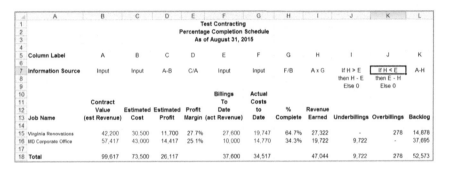

	A	B	C	D	E	F	G	H	I	J	K	L
1						Test Contracting						
2						Percentage Completion Schedule						
3						As of August 31, 2015						
4												
5	Column Label	A	B	C	D	E	F	G	H	I	J	K
6												
7	Information Source	Input	Input	A-B	C/A	Input	Input	F/B	A x G	If H > E then H - E Else 0	If H < E then E - H Else 0	A-H
8												
9												
10						Billings	Actual					
11			Contract			To	Costs					
12			Value	Estimated	Estimated	Profit	Date	to	%	Revenue		
13	Job Name		(est Revenue)	Cost	Profit	Margin	(act Revenue)	Date	Complete	Earned	Underbillings	Overbillings	Backlog
14												
15	Virginia Renovations		42,200	30,500	11,700	27.7%	27,600	19,747	64.7%	27,322	-	278	14,878
16	MD Corporate Office		57,417	43,000	14,417	25.1%	10,000	14,770	34.3%	19,722	9,722	-	37,695
17												
18	Total		99,617	73,500	26,117		37,600	34,517		47,044	9,722	278	52,573

A few notes on the spreadsheet:

- Information Source (row 7) acts as a legend to the information below it—the columns noted as "Input" contain the data brought over from QuickBooks; remaining are the equations applied to the data in those columns.
- The term "Underbillings" is a short name for "Costs and Estimated Earnings in Excess of Billings," which is shown as a current asset on the balance sheet.
- The term "Overbillings" is a short name for "Billings in Excess of Costs and Estimated Earnings," which is shown as a current liability on the balance sheet.
- The Backlog amount is a figure that banks and surety companies like to see on these schedules because it represents the remaining revenue to be earned on a contract. This is calculated as the difference between the contract value and revenue earned to date.

A percentage completion spreadsheet can also be set up to prepare the required journal entry that records the adjustment to revenue. Below is the journal entry for the above example.

	Journal Entry to Record:	Debit	Credit
21	Journal Entry to Record:	Debit	Credit
22			
23	Job Income - Virginia Renovations	278	
24	Billings in Excess of Costs and Estimated Earnings		278
25			
26	Costs and Estimated Earnings in Excess of Billings	9,722	
27	Job Income - MD Corporate Office		9,722

A review of your percentage completion schedule for errors and information needing investigation is highly recommended. Some trouble areas to watch for:

- If there is a Profit Margin that is outside of the norm for your company, it is likely that the Contract Value or Estimated Cost is in error.
- Billings to Date should not exceed the total Contract Value. If this is the case, investigate if the Contract Value needs to be updated for change orders or if there is a billing error.
- Costs to Date should not exceed total Estimated Costs; this would produce a % Complete exceeding 100%. Evaluate if the costs posted to the job are correct or if the Cost Estimate needs to be increased.
- Review the completion percentages on the schedule with your project managers. If, for example, the schedule indicates a job is 90% complete while the project manager on the job says it is only 50% complete, something is obviously amiss.

Notes:

_____

_____

_____

_____

_____

_____

_____

_____

_____

_____

_____

_____

_____

_____

_____

_____

_____

_____

_____

_____

_____

_____

_____

_____

_____

_____

_____

_____

_____

_____

_____

_____

_____

_____

_____

_____

Chapter Eleven

Functionality for Government Contractors

Under many government contracts, companies must aggregate various levels of cost and allocate costs to contracts to justify billing rates and secure payment. This chapter will explain the functionality available in QuickBooks for grouping or aggregating costs, allocating costs, and determining whether allocations are over or under applied. The specifics of which costs *are* or *are not* allowed to be grouped and the basis for acceptable cost allocation is outside the scope of this course.

Costs Aggregation Approaches

Account Types

Account types are the highest level of segregation in the QuickBooks Chart of Accounts. QuickBooks provides two account types for income/revenue and three for costs. Account types are fixed; the titles cannot be changed, nor can additional types be added. Profit and Loss account types are as follows, along with their typical use:

Income/Revenue

- Income – Revenues billed/earned in the normal course of business
- Other Income – nonrecurring items such as gains on sale of equipment, proceeds from legal settlements, and earnings on investments

Costs/Expenses

- Cost of Goods Sold – costs directly attributable to revenues, i.e. "Job Cost"
- Expenses – costs typically considered overhead
- Other Expense – nonrecurring items such as losses on sale of equipment, legal settlements, and investments (Many government contractors use the Other Expense category to group costs considered "unallowable" under federal acquisition regulations.)

Accounts & Sub Accounts

In a manner similar to the approach for equipment costing in Chapter Eight, costs to be allocated are set up as sub accounts under a parent account. It is possible to have as many as five layers of sub accounts in QuickBooks. Costs are charged to these accounts, which forms "cost pools."

Costs are allocated from the cost pool to jobs using two accounts: one for the charge to jobs and the other to reduce, or zero out, the cost pool. As with equipment costing, this enables the user to see if costs have been over or under applied.

Class Codes

For contractors with larger organizations, class codes provide another level to segregate revenues and costs in QuickBooks. Typically, class codes are used as a department, location, or profit/cost center code. For class codes to be used, it must be turned on as a preference.

To set the preference:

1. On the main menu, go to Edit.
2. Select Preferences.
3. Choose the Accounting Preference.
4. Select both "Use class transactions for Preferences" and "Prompt to assign classes" options.

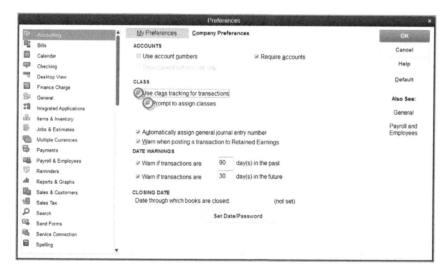

Profit and Loss statements can be run by class code and expenses not assigned class codes will appear in a column labeled "Unclassified."

Cost Allocation Approaches

As shown in Chapter Eight, allocation of overhead and other costs to jobs can be done either with a journal entry or the zero-dollar bill approach.

Notes:

Chapter Twelve

Reports

QuickBooks provides numerous reports for analyzing profitability at summary and detailed levels. In addition, there are reports that can highlight errors made in recording and processing transactions. Reports can be customized in several ways, and then "memorized" for future use. In this section, the standard reports will be reviewed and techniques for customization discussed. These reports are found in the Jobs, Time & Mileage section of Reports.

Reports to Review for Data Integrity

Expenses Not Assigned to Jobs

Before running job reports, it's a good idea to see if any costs that should have been charged to jobs were not coded with a job code. This is easily done by running the Expenses Not Assigned to Jobs report. Expenses appearing on the report should be edited if they should in fact be assigned to specific jobs. This report may be found in different menu options depending on the version of QuickBooks you are using.

Below is a sample report.

Quality-Built Construction
Expenses Not Assigned to Jobs
October 1 - 19, 2019

Type	Date	Num	Memo	Account	Class	Amount
Acme Fast Fuel						
Credit Card Cha...	10/01/2019	CC		Gas & Oil		15.00 ◀
Check	10/02/2019	Cash		Gas & Oil		32.00
Total Acme Fast Fuel						47.00
All Star Truck Sales						
Bill	10/09/2019		Service AC	Repairs & Mainten...		1,230.00
Total All Star Truck Sales						1,230.00
Big-Value Warehouse Store						
Bill	10/02/2019			Office Supplies		72.00
Bill	10/09/2019			Office Supplies		72.00
Bill	10/16/2019			Office Supplies		72.00
Total Big-Value Warehouse Store						216.00
Debbie's Deli						
Credit Card Cha...	10/08/2019	CC		Meals and Enterta...		23.95
Total Debbie's Deli						23.95

Unbilled Costs by Job

For contractors using the Time and Material billing functionality, this report details items of expense that have not been billed. The report is first sorted by job, then by vendor. An example:

Test Contracting, LLC
Unbilled Costs by Job
All Transactions

Type	Date	Source Name	Memo	Account	Billing Status	Amount
ABC, Inc.						
Virginia Renovations						
Paycheck	07/17/2015	Harold S Jones		Workers Compens...	Unbilled	36.40 ◀
Paycheck	07/17/2015	John T Smith		Workers Compens...	Unbilled	46.02
Bill	07/27/2015	B & B Brick and B...		Subcontractors Co...	Unbilled	500.00
Paycheck	08/01/2015	Harold S Jones		Workers Compens...	Unbilled	18.20
Paycheck	08/01/2015	John T Smith		Workers Compens...	Unbilled	15.34
Bill	01/31/2016	Allocation Vendor		Job Equipment Cost	Unbilled	4,250.00
Total Virginia Renovations						4,865.96
Total ABC, Inc.						4,865.96
Acme Supermarkets						
New Building						
Bill	07/27/2015	Sunoco	Excavation	Subcontractors Co...	Unbilled	500.00
Total New Building						500.00
Total Acme Supermarkets						500.00
XYZ Company						
MD Corporate Office						
Paycheck	07/17/2015	Harold S Jones		Workers Compens...	Unbilled	46.20
Paycheck	07/17/2015	John T Smith		Workers Compens...	Unbilled	25.96
Paycheck	08/01/2015	Harold S Jones		Workers Compens...	Unbilled	23.10
Paycheck	08/01/2015	John T Smith		Workers Compens...	Unbilled	19.47
General Journal	01/31/2016	ABC, Inc. Virginia...	allocate equ...	Job Equipment Cost	Unbilled	6,500.00
Bill	01/31/2016	Allocation Vendor		Job Equipment Cost	Unbilled	6,500.00
Total MD Corporate Office						13,114.73

Job Profitability Reports

QuickBooks has numerous reports that enable the contractor to review the profitability of jobs at either the detailed level or summary level. In this section the reports available to the contractor will be reviewed.

Summary Profitability Reporting

For a high level look at jobs, the Job Profitability Report shows Total Billing, Total Costs, and the difference, sorted by customer, then job. While the default time period is All, it can be modified to show specific time periods. This report can be a quick way to spot problem jobs. For example, jobs showing large losses or no revenue can be flagged for more detailed review. Below is the report from a sample company. To run this report, begin at the main menu and select Reports, Jobs, Time & Mileage, then Job Profitability Summary.

Quality-Built Construction
Job Profitability Summary
All Transactions

	Act. Cost	Act. Revenue	($) Diff.
ABC Company			
Concrete Floor	2,050.00	4,950.00	2,900.00
Total ABC Company	2,050.00	4,950.00	2,900.00
Mr & Mrs Jones			
Kitchen Remodel	0.00	5,000.00	5,000.00
Total Mr & Mrs Jones	0.00	5,000.00	5,000.00
James Smith			
New Kitchen	14,375.00	20,000.00	5,625.00
Total James Smith	14,375.00	20,000.00	5,625.00
Campbell, Heather			
House-New Construction	143,468.05	207,682.50	64,214.45
Total Campbell, Heather	143,468.05	207,682.50	64,214.45
Cruz, Albert			
Kitchen Remodel	129,915.40	225,000.00	95,084.60
Cottage - New Construction	203,043.46	301,500.00	98,456.54
Total Cruz, Albert	332,958.86	526,500.00	193,541.14
Hamby, Shane			
Cottage - New Construction	84,479.04	135,640.00	51,160.96
Total Hamby, Shane	84,479.04	135,640.00	51,160.96
Molotsi, Hugh			
Second Story Addition	318,497.19	447,500.00	129,002.81
Total Molotsi, Hugh	318,497.19	447,500.00	129,002.81
Quality-Built Construction			
Admin/Paperwork	71,665.53	0.00	-71,665.53
Bidding	16,588.43	0.00	-16,588.43

To show the drill down capability and reports that can be used, The Albert Cruz Cottage – New Construction job has been highlighted above, and we'll be showing other reports with varying degrees of detail for this job below.

© The CFO Source, LLC 2015

Individual Job Profitability Reports

Several reports are available in QuickBooks that allow a "drill down" to the job detail level. Which of these reports will be most useful depends on two things:

- Whether expenses are recorded at the item code level or the expenses level
- Whether the job estimates are input into QuickBooks

Profit and Loss by Job

This report is useful regardless of whether item codes are used for expenses, or estimates are input into QuickBooks. The report shows actual revenues and expenses for the time period selected with no reporting on the estimate side. This is an excellent report for those contractors who do not want to incur the expense and effort of inputting estimates.

From the main menu, select Reports, Jobs, Time & Mileage, then Profit and Loss by Job. When this report is run, it shows all jobs for the time period selected. To run the report for only one job, it must be filtered for just that job. (Filtering reports will be covered later in this section.)

Below is the report for the Albert Cruz Cottage – New Construction job, highlighted in the last image. Note that expenses on the job are shown in both the Cost of Goods Sold and Expenses sections of the report. The same information appears in all columns of the report because the report is designed to be run for multiple jobs; the two columns on the right are subtotals of the overall report level when the report is filtered down to only one job.

Quality-Built Construction
Profit & Loss by Job
All Transactions

	Cottage - New Construction (Cruz, Albert)	Total Cruz, Albert	TOTAL
Ordinary Income/Expense			
Income			
4110 · Construction Income	301,500.00	301,500.00	301,500.00
Total Income	301,500.00	301,500.00	301,500.00
Cost of Goods Sold			
5110 · Job Related Costs	82,431.99	82,431.99	82,431.99
5200 · Job Labor Costs			
5210 · Job Labor (Gross Wages)	40,704.50	40,704.50	40,704.50
5220 · Worker's Compensation C...	3,928.77	3,928.77	3,928.77
5230 · Direct Payroll Taxes	0.00	0.00	0.00
5200 · Job Labor Costs - Other	6,903.40	6,903.40	6,903.40
Total 5200 · Job Labor Costs	51,536.67	51,536.67	51,536.67
5300 · Materials	27,248.00	27,248.00	27,248.00
5400 · Subcontractors	40,491.00	40,491.00	40,491.00
5950 · Other Job Costs	125.00	125.00	125.00
Total COGS	201,832.66	201,832.66	201,832.66
Gross Profit	99,667.34	99,667.34	99,667.34
Expense			
▶ 6180 · Insurance	10.80	10.80	10.80
▶ 6500 · Payroll Expenses (office)	1,200.00	1,200.00	1,200.00
Total Expense	1,210.80	1,210.80	1,210.80
Net Ordinary Income	98,456.54	98,456.54	98,456.54
Net Income	98,456.54	98,456.54	98,456.54

Job Profitability Detail

Only useful if expenses have been recorded at the item code level, this report shows spending details. Below is the report for the same job reported above.

Quality-Built Construction			
Job Profitability Detail for Cruz, Albert:Cottage - New Construction			
All Transactions			
	Act. Cost	Act. Revenue	($) Diff.
04 Concrete (Concrete)	1,204.55	0.00	-1,204.55
05 Masonry (Masonry)	1,438.84	0.00	-1,438.84
06 Floor Framing (Floor Framing)	5,728.12	0.00	-5,728.12
07 Wall Framing (Wall Framing)	7,375.10	0.00	-7,375.10
08 Roof Framing (Roof Framing)	9,071.35	0.00	-9,071.35
09 Roof Flashing (Roof Flashing)	2,112.47	0.00	-2,112.47
10 Exterior Trim & Decks (Exterior Trim & De...	4,314.68	0.00	-4,314.68
11 Siding (Siding)	2,989.20	0.00	-2,989.20
12 Doors & Trim (Doors & Trim)	13,515.36	0.00	-13,515.36
13 Windows & Trim (Windows & Trim)	5,096.45	0.00	-5,096.45
14 Plumbing (Plumbing)	36,755.37	0.00	-36,755.37
15 HVAC (Heating & Cooling)	25,793.04	0.00	-25,793.04
16 Electrical & Lighting (Electrical & Lighting)	5,978.83	0.00	-5,978.83
17 Insulation (Insulation)	2,897.45	0.00	-2,897.45
18 Interior Walls (Interior Walls)	7,098.58	0.00	-7,098.58
19 Ceilings & Cover (Ceilings & Coverings)	2,107.09	0.00	-2,107.09
20 Millwork & Trim (Millwork & Trim)	2,107.07	0.00	-2,107.07
21 Cabinets & Vanities (Cabinets & Vanities)	25,790.77	0.00	-25,790.77
22 Specialty	7,929.90	0.00	-7,929.90
23 Floor Coverings (Floor Coverings)	6,985.07	0.00	-6,985.07
24 Paint (Painting)	4,332.15	0.00	-4,332.15
25 Cleanup (Cleanup & Restoration)	4,565.31	0.00	-4,565.31
26 Landscape & Paving (Landscape & Paving)	13,224.33	0.00	-13,224.33
FP Billing (__% due upon completion of ___.)	0.00	301,500.00	301,500.00
Total Service	203,043.46	301,500.00	98,456.54
TOTAL	203,043.46	301,500.00	98,456.54

Job Estimates vs. Actuals Detail

This is the most useful report for job cost analysis in QuickBooks, allowing the contractor to compare each line item in an estimate against actual spending. Such analysis is critical in successfully managing current jobs and estimating future jobs. In order to use this report, estimates must be created for jobs and expenses must be recorded using item codes. Below is the report for the same job shown above.

Quality-Built Construction

Job Estimates vs. Actuals Detail for Cruz, Albert:Cottage - New Construction

All Transactions

	Est. Cost	Act. Cost	($) Diff.	Est. Revenue	Act. Revenue	($) Diff.
04 Concrete (Concrete)	1,000.00	1,204.55	204.55	1,000.00	0.00	-1,000.00
05 Masonry (Masonry)	1,500.00	1,438.84	-61.16	1,500.00	0.00	-1,500.00
06 Floor Framing (Floor Framing)	6,000.00	5,728.12	-271.88	6,000.00	0.00	-6,000.00
07 Wall Framing (Wall Framing)	7,000.00	7,375.10	375.10	7,000.00	0.00	-7,000.00
08 Roof Framing (Roof Framing)	9,000.00	9,071.35	71.35	9,000.00	0.00	-9,000.00
09 Roof Flashing (Roof Flashing)	3,000.00	2,112.47	-887.53	3,000.00	0.00	-3,000.00
10 Exterior Trim & Decks (Exterior Trim & De...	5,000.00	4,314.68	-685.32	5,000.00	0.00	-5,000.00
11 Siding (Siding)	3,000.00	2,989.20	-10.80	3,000.00	0.00	-3,000.00
12 Doors & Trim (Doors & Trim)	14,000.00	13,515.36	-484.64	14,000.00	0.00	-14,000.00
13 Windows & Trim (Windows & Trim)	5,000.00	5,096.45	96.45	5,000.00	0.00	-5,000.00
14 Plumbing (Plumbing)	38,000.00	36,755.37	-1,244.63	38,000.00	0.00	-38,000.00
15 HVAC (Heating & Cooling)	27,000.00	25,793.04	-1,206.96	27,000.00	0.00	-27,000.00
16 Electrical & Lighting (Electrical & Lighting)	6,000.00	5,978.83	-21.17	6,000.00	0.00	-6,000.00
17 Insulation (Insulation)	3,000.00	2,897.45	-102.55	3,000.00	0.00	-3,000.00
18 Interior Walls (Interior Walls)	6,000.00	7,098.58	1,098.58	6,000.00	0.00	-6,000.00
19 Ceilings & Cover (Ceilings & Coverings)	2,000.00	2,107.09	107.09	2,000.00	0.00	-2,000.00
20 Millwork & Trim (Millwork & Trim)	2,000.00	2,107.07	107.07	2,000.00	0.00	-2,000.00
21 Cabinets & Vanities (Cabinets & Vanities)	26,000.00	25,790.77	-209.23	26,000.00	0.00	-26,000.00
22 Specialty	8,000.00	7,929.90	-70.10	8,000.00	0.00	-8,000.00
23 Floor Coverings (Floor Coverings)	6,000.00	6,985.07	985.07	6,000.00	0.00	-6,000.00
24 Paint (Painting)	4,000.00	4,332.15	332.15	4,000.00	0.00	-4,000.00
25 Cleanup (Cleanup & Restoration)	3,000.00	4,565.31	1,565.31	3,000.00	0.00	-3,000.00
26 Landscape & Paving (Landscape & Paving)	10,000.00	13,224.33	3,224.33	10,000.00	0.00	-10,000.00
FP Billing (__% due upon completion of ___.)	0.00	0.00	0.00	0.00	301,500.00	301,500.00
Total Service	198,825.00	203,043.46	4,218.46	198,825.00	301,500.00	102,675.00
TOTAL	198,825.00	203,043.46	4,218.46	198,825.00	301,500.00	102,675.00

Modifying and Memorizing Reports

QuickBooks not only provides users with a wide selection of reports, but it also provides the user with numerous ways to modify reports for making them more useful. After running a report from the main menu Reports option, the user has a wide variety of tools available to customize the report in numerous ways. These include establishing date ranges, presentation formats, filtering for selected criteria, and summarizing data.

The Expand/Collapse Function

This functionality allows the user to toggle back and forth between more or less detail on the same report. On financial statements, sub accounts can be either shown in detail (in the Expand mode) or collapsed to a summary (in the Collapse mode). Shown below is a Profit and Loss in the Expand format, so sub accounts are shown.

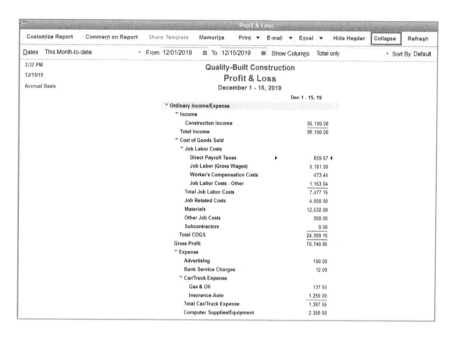

Here's the same report after toggling to Expand:

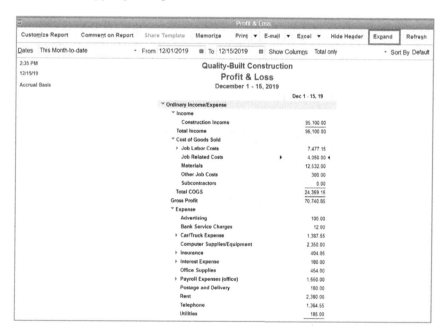

On the Collapsed Report, the sub accounts do not appear, only the totals in the main accounts.

The user also has the option of choosing to collapse some subaccounts into the parent account while leaving other accounts in detail. This is done by clicking on the small grey arrows to the left of the accounts. Below is a hybrid of the two examples above:

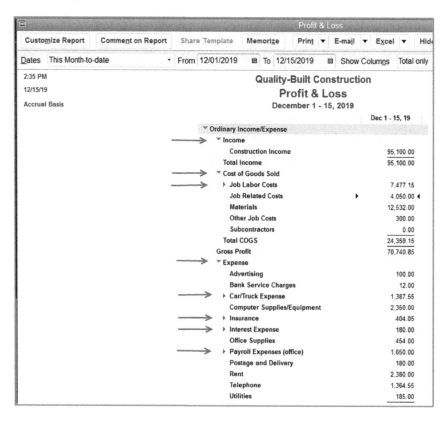

Customizing Reports

After the report is displayed, click on the Customize Report tab in the report menu as shown below:

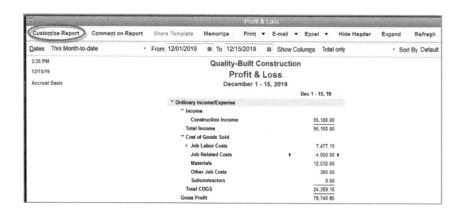

This brings up the Modify Report screen with four tabs, each having different functionality.

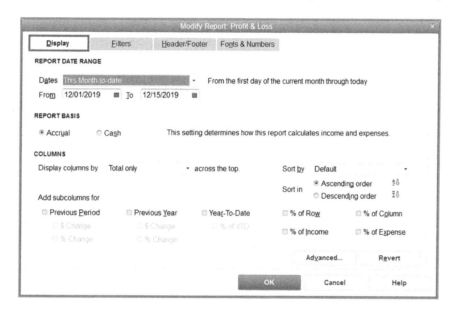

In the Display options tab, the user can:

- select a date range;
- choose Accrual or Cash Reporting; (the default for this can be set in the Reports and Graphs Preference section)
- display by time period (week, month, quarter) or data field, such as class;
- click the advanced button on the bottom to select whether zeroes should be shown.

Selecting the Filters Tab brings up the following screen:

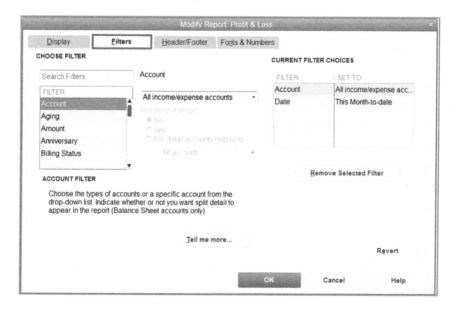

In the Filters options tab, the user can:

- choose from one or multiple data fields to filter the report;
- filter for one or more attributes for each data field that is selected.

For example, a report could be filtered for only income (sales) accounts, then also filtered for specific names (Customers).

Selecting the Header/Footer tab brings up the following screen:

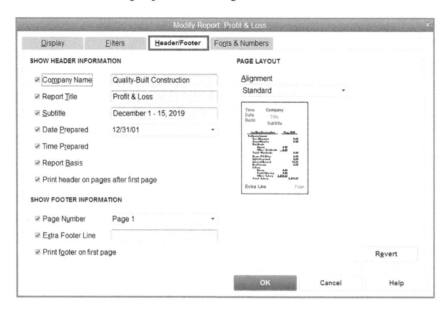

In this tab, the user can alter the standard header and footer titles for the report, add page numbers, and change the alignment in preparation for printing.

Selecting the Fonts & Numbers tab brings up the following screen:

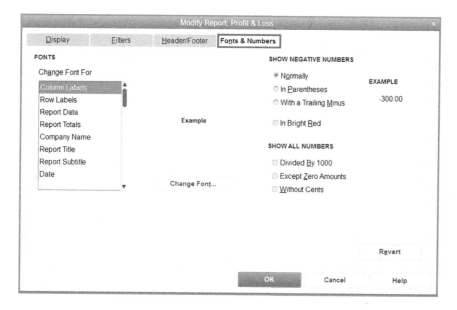

In this tab, the user can select:

- how negative numbers will be displayed;
- to show cents or round to thousands;
- change the font of selected label.

Memorizing (and Retrieving) Reports

After getting a report just the way you want it, you can save the report for later use by clicking on the Memorize tab in the report menu.

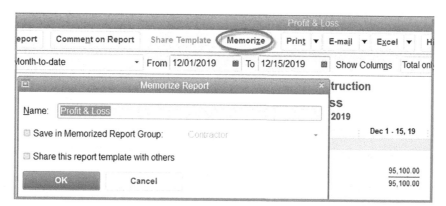

This brings up the Memorize Report box where you can give your report a name. Once saved, memorized reports can be brought up by selecting the Memorized Reports option under Reports on the main menu.

© The CFO Source, LLC 2015

Notes:

Notes:

Appendix A

Standard QuickBooks Contractor Item Code List

Item	Description
01 Plans and Permits	Plans and Permits
01 Plans and Permits:01.1 Plans	Plans
01 Plans and Permits:01.2 Building Permits	Building Permits
01 Plans and Permits:01.3 City License	City License Fee
02 Site Work	Site Work
02 Site Work:02.10 Demo	Demo
03 Excavation	Excavation
04 Concrete	Concrete
05 Masonry	Masonry
06 Floor Frame	Floor Framing
07 Wall Frame	Wall Framing
08 Roof Frame	Roof Framing
09 Roof Flashing	Roofing, Flashing
10 Exterior Trim & Decks	Exterior Trim & Decks
11 Siding	Siding
12 Doors & Trim	Doors & Trim
13 Windows & Trim	Windows & Trim
14 Plumbing	Plumbing
15 HVAC	Heating & Cooling
16 Electrical & Lighting	Electrical & Lighting
17 Insulation	Insulation
18 Interior Walls	Interior Walls
19 Ceilings & Cover	Ceilings & Coverings
20 Millwork & Trim	Millwork & Trim
21 Cabinets & Vanities	Cabinets & Vanities
22 Specialty	Specialties
23 Floor Coverings	Floor Coverings
24 Paint	Painting
25 Cleanup	Cleanup & Restoration
26 Landscaping & Paving	26 Landscaping & Paving
27 Contingency	Contingency
28 Commissions	Sales Commisions
29 Supervision	Supervision
30 Finance	Job Loan Costs

Appendix B

Suggested General Conditions Item Codes

Sub item	COGS Account
Bonds	Bonds
Meals	Meals
Licenses and Permits	Licenses and Permits
Cleaning	Other Job Costs
Fencing	Other Job Costs
Job site trailer	Other Job Costs
Job site utilities	Other Job Costs
Landfill Fees/Trash Removal	Other Job Costs
Mob/Demob	Other Job Costs
Photography	Other Job Costs
Plans/Specs	Other Job Costs
Portable Toilet	Other Job Costs
Safety	Other Job Costs
Security	Other Job Costs
Signage	Other Job Costs
Small Tools	Other Job Costs
Storage	Other Job Costs
Supplies	Other Job Costs
Tolls/Parking	Other Job Costs
Travel	Other Job Costs

Appendix C

Suggested Item Code List for Subcontractors		
Item	**Sub item**	**COGS Account**
Supervisory Labor		Supervisory Labor
Direct Labor	St Time	Direct Labor - St Time
	OT	Direct Labor - OT
Labor Burden	PR Taxes	Payroll Taxes
	Workers Comp	Workers Comp
	Co Paid Benefits	Fringes
Temporary Labor		Temorary Labor
Materials	breakdowns as desired	Materials
	breakdowns as desired	Materials
	breakdowns as desired	Materials
	breakdowns as desired	Materials
	breakdowns as desired	Materials
Subcontractors		Subcontractors
Equipment Rentals		Equipment Rentals
Equipment/Vehicle Cost Allocations		Equipment Cost Allocation

Need More Help?

QuickBooks is a feature rich product that can provide valuable reports and information. Knowing all the functionality that is available and how to implement it can create a real advantage for improving cash flow and profitability. At The CFO Source, we work with clients to help them get the most from QuickBooks. With our years of experience as CFOs, Controllers, and QuickBooks Pro Advisors, you can realize a very positive impact for your business in a short period of time.

The CFO Source's QuickBooks Consulting services will help you:

- select the right version – Enterprise, Premier, Pro, or On-line;

- determine where to set up QuickBooks – local server, cloud provider, desktop;

- create chart of accounts and item codes setups tailored to your business;

- set up estimate versus actual reporting for jobs;

- train staff, making them QuickBooks gurus;

- use the data condense function to speed up your QuickBooks;

- convert from other accounting software;

- select and use "Add on" third party programs that link to QuickBooks;

- set up different levels of access for users in a multi-user environment;

- export large amounts of data to Excel for analytics, such as pivot tables;

- turn on or off functionality by customizing preference settings;

- train on techniques to improve data quality and limit input errors;

- customize invoices with your logo, contact info, and messages;

- and much more!

The CFO Source's Construction Industry and CFO services will help you:

- set up estimating spreadsheets customized to your business;

- prepare percentage completion accounting to satisfy your banks and sureties;

- monthly or quarterly review of your accounting;

- budgeting and cash flow forecasting;

- analyze new business ventures, acquisitions, and major purchases;

- arrange equipment and working capital financing;

- calculate your true hourly cost of labor, factoring in all costs – base pay, payroll taxes, worker's comp, company paid benefits, and paid time off;

- tax planning and preparation of personal and corporate tax returns;

- outsourced payroll and bookkeeping services utilizing your QB or ours;

- and much more!

We can be found at www.cfosource.net, or feel free to call us at 410-242-0526. We utilize the latest in remote access tools for clients who are not local. Contact us today and let's get QuickBooks providing the information you need to make your company successful.

CPSIA information can be obtained
at www.ICGtesting.com
Printed in the USA
LVOW06s0905080517
533681LV00011B/22/P